Modern Critical Views

Chinua Achebe
Henry Adams
Aeschylus
S. Y. Agnon
Edward Albee
Raphael Alberti
Louisa May Alcott
A. R. Ammons
Sherwood Anderson
Aristophanes
Matthew Arnold
Antonin Artaud
John Ashbery
Margaret Atwood
W. H. Auden
Jane Austen
Isaac Babel
Sir Francis Bacon
James Baldwin
Honoré de Balzac
John Barth
Donald Barthelme
Charles Baudelaire
Simone de Beauvoir
Samuel Beckett
Saul Bellow
Thomas Berger
John Berryman
The Bible
Elizabeth Bishop
William Blake
Giovanni Boccaccio
Heinrich Böll
Jorge Luis Borges
Elizabeth Bowen
Bertolt Brecht
The Brontës
Charles Brockden Brown
Sterling Brown
Robert Browning
Martin Buber
John Bunyan
Anthony Burgess
Kenneth Burke
Robert Burns
William Burroughs
George Gordon, Lord
   Byron
Pedro Calderón de la Barca
Italo Calvino
Albert Camus
Canadian Poetry: Modern
   and Contemporary
Canadian Poetry through
   E. J. Pratt
Thomas Carlyle
Alejo Carpentier
Lewis Carroll
Willa Cather
Louis-Ferdinand Céline
Miguel de Cervantes

Geoffrey Chaucer
John Cheever
Anton Chekhov
Kate Chopin
Chrétien de Troyes
Agatha Christie
Samuel Taylor Coleridge
Colette
William Congreve & the
   Restoration Dramatists
Joseph Conrad
Contemporary Poets
James Fenimore Cooper
Pierre Corneille
Julio Cortázar
Hart Crane
Stephen Crane
e. e. cummings
Dante
Robertson Davies
Daniel Defoe
Philip K. Dick
Charles Dickens
James Dickey
Emily Dickinson
Denis Diderot
Isak Dinesen
E. L. Doctorow
John Donne & the
   Seventeenth-Century
   Metaphysical Poets
John Dos Passos
Fyodor Dostoevsky
Frederick Douglass
Theodore Dreiser
John Dryden
W. E. B. Du Bois
Lawrence Durrell
George Eliot
T. S. Eliot
Elizabethan Dramatists
Ralph Ellison
Ralph Waldo Emerson
Euripides
William Faulkner
Henry Fielding
F. Scott Fitzgerald
Gustave Flaubert
E. M. Forster
John Fowles
Sigmund Freud
Robert Frost
Northrop Frye
Carlos Fuentes
William Gaddis
Federico García Lorca
Gabriel García Márquez
André Gide
W. S. Gilbert
Allen Ginsberg
J. W. von Goethe

Nikolai Gogol
William Golding
Oliver Goldsmith
Mary Gordon
Günther Grass
Robert Graves
Graham Greene
Thomas Hardy
Nathaniel Hawthorne
William Hazlitt
H. D.
Seamus Heaney
Lillian Hellman
Ernest Hemingway
Hermann Hesse
Geoffrey Hill
Friedrich Hölderlin
Homer
A. D. Hope
Gerard Manley Hopkins
Horace
A. E. Housman
William Dean Howells
Langston Hughes
Ted Hughes
Victor Hugo
Zora Neale Hurston
Aldous Huxley
Henrik Ibsen
Eugène Ionesco
Washington Irving
Henry James
Dr. Samuel Johnson and
   James Boswell
Ben Jonson
James Joyce
Carl Gustav Jung
Franz Kafka
Yasonari Kawabata
John Keats
Søren Kierkegaard
Rudyard Kipling
Melanie Klein
Heinrich von Kleist
Philip Larkin
D. H. Lawrence
John le Carré
Ursula K. Le Guin
Giacomo Leopardi
Doris Lessing
Sinclair Lewis
Jack London
Robert Lowell
Malcolm Lowry
Carson McCullers
Norman Mailer
Bernard Malamud
Stéphane Mallarmé
Sir Thomas Malory
André Malraux
Thomas Mann

Modern Critical Views

Katherine Mansfield
Christopher Marlowe
Andrew Marvell
Herman Melville
George Meredith
James Merrill
John Stuart Mill
Arthur Miller
Henry Miller
John Milton
Yukio Mishima
Molière
Michel de Montaigne
Eugenio Montale
Marianne Moore
Alberto Moravia
Toni Morrison
Alice Munro
Iris Murdoch
Robert Musil
Vladimir Nabokov
V. S. Naipaul
R. K. Narayan
Pablo Neruda
John Henry Newman
Friedrich Nietzsche
Frank Norris
Joyce Carol Oates
Sean O'Casey
Flannery O'Connor
Christopher Okigbo
Charles Olson
Eugene O'Neill
José Ortega y Gasset
Joe Orton
George Orwell
Ovid
Wilfred Owen
Amos Oz
Cynthia Ozick
Grace Paley
Blaise Pascal
Walter Pater
Octavio Paz
Walker Percy
Petrarch
Pindar
Harold Pinter
Luigi Pirandello
Sylvia Plath
Plato

Plautus
Edgar Allan Poe
Poets of Sensibility & the Sublime
Poets of the Nineties
Alexander Pope
Katherine Anne Porter
Ezra Pound
Anthony Powell
Pre-Raphaelite Poets
Marcel Proust
Manuel Puig
Alexander Pushkin
Thomas Pynchon
Francisco de Quevedo
François Rabelais
Jean Racine
Ishmael Reed
Adrienne Rich
Samuel Richardson
Mordecai Richler
Rainer Maria Rilke
Arthur Rimbaud
Edwin Arlington Robinson
Theodore Roethke
Philip Roth
Jean-Jacques Rousseau
John Ruskin
J. D. Salinger
Jean-Paul Sartre
Gershom Scholem
Sir Walter Scott
William Shakespeare
  Histories & Poems
  Comedies & Romances
  Tragedies
George Bernard Shaw
Mary Wollstonecraft Shelley
Percy Bysshe Shelley
Sam Shepard
Richard Brinsley Sheridan
Sir Philip Sidney
Isaac Bashevis Singer
Tobias Smollett
Alexander Solzhenitsyn
Sophocles
Wole Soyinka
Edmund Spenser
Gertrude Stein
John Steinbeck

Stendhal
Laurence Sterne
Wallace Stevens
Robert Louis Stevenson
Tom Stoppard
August Strindberg
Jonathan Swift
John Millington Synge
Alfred, Lord Tennyson
William Makepeace Thackeray
Dylan Thomas
Henry David Thoreau
James Thurber and S. J. Perelman
J. R. R. Tolkien
Leo Tolstoy
Jean Toomer
Lionel Trilling
Anthony Trollope
Ivan Turgenev
Mark Twain
Miguel de Unamuno
John Updike
Paul Valéry
Cesar Vallejo
Lope de Vega
Gore Vidal
Virgil
Voltaire
Kurt Vonnegut
Derek Walcott
Alice Walker
Robert Penn Warren
Evelyn Waugh
H. G. Wells
Eudora Welty
Nathanael West
Edith Wharton
Patrick White
Walt Whitman
Oscar Wilde
Tennessee Williams
William Carlos Williams
Thomas Wolfe
Virginia Woolf
William Wordsworth
Jay Wright
Richard Wright
William Butler Yeats
A. B. Yehoshua
Emile Zola

Modern Critical Views

FLANNERY O'CONNOR

Edited and with an introduction by
Harold Bloom
Sterling Professor of the Humanities
Yale University

CHELSEA HOUSE PUBLISHERS
New York ◊ Philadelphia

10   9   8   7   6   5   4   3

∞ The paper used in this publication meets the minimum
requirements of the American National Standard for Permanence of Paper for Printed Library Materials, Z39.48–1984.

Library of Congress Cataloging-in-Publication Data
Flannery O'Connor.
    (Modern critical views)
    Bibliography: p.
    Includes index.
    1. O'Connor, Flannery — Criticism and interpretation —
Addresses, essays, lectures.   I. Bloom, Harold.
II. Series.
PR3565.C57Z6678   1986   813'.54   86–2676
ISBN 0–87754–632–0

Contents

Editor's Note

This book brings together the best criticism available upon the stories and novels of Flannery O'Connor, arranged in the chronological order of its publication. I am grateful to David Parker for his aid in researching this volume.

The introduction centers upon *The Violent Bear It Away,* and two stories, "A Good Man Is Hard to Find" and "A View of the Woods," in order to explore what many readers have found to be a division between O'Connor's stance as a Catholic moralist, and the extraordinary thematic and narrative violence of her characteristic work. John Hawkes, distinguished novelist and friend of O'Connor, shrewdly links her to Nathanael West's parallel preoccupation with violence and the sacred, in an essay that begins the chronological sequence of criticism here. In the first of his two appearances in this book, the late Robert Fitzgerald, admirable poet and close friend of O'Connor, gives an exemplary reading to the story "The Displaced Person," which is followed by his poignant and illuminating introduction to *Everything That Rises Must Converge.*

An analysis of O'Connor's first novel, *Wise Blood,* by Lewis A. Lawson concludes that her peculiar mode of the grotesque resulted from her conviction that a world which had abandoned normative religion could only be represented without norms, as wholly fallen into the grotesque. Joyce Carol Oates, herself a visionary storyteller of singular power and persuasiveness, describes O'Connor's visionary art as a pure kind of revelation, archaic and sublime, impatient of the codification of apocalyptic religious experience into dogma.

In a reading of O'Connor's first and last stories, Ralph C. Wood convincingly affirms that the spiritual and aesthetic distance traversed between "The Geranium" and "Judgement Day" is a matter not of decades but of light years. Carol Shloss, analyzing several major stories, concludes that they are epiphanies, deliberately leaving nothing to inference. Confirmation of this argument is offered by Ronald Schleifer's more secular contention that the supernatural interventions crowding O'Connor's "rural Gothic" allow the author to transcend the more inadequate tropes to which her rhetoric sometimes submits. Another kind of confirmation is presented in the exegesis of the Double motif in O'Connor by Frederick Asals, which discovers transcendent aspects that mitigate the obsessiveness of this recurrent element in her work.

Two powerful advanced critiques of O'Connor end this volume, with each highly aware of the Gnostic auras so strangely present in her work, and each deeply informed by current developments in literary criticism. Jefferson Humphries relates O'Connor both to Proust and to the aesthetic of violence, each pervaded by Gnostic images, while John Burt analyzes *Wise Blood* and the great, somber story "Parker's Back" as instances of her most authentic spiritual vision, with Gnostic and even Calvinist overtones. Both Humphries and Burt carry us full circle back to the editor's introduction, with its meditation upon what may be incongruous in O'Connor's theology in regard to her actual narrative art.

Introduction

A professedly Roman Catholic prose romance begins with the death of an eighty-four-year-old Southern American Protestant, self-called prophet, and professional moonshiner, as set forth in this splendidly comprehensive sentence:

> Francis Marion Tarwater's uncle had been dead for only half a day when the boy got too drunk to finish digging his grave and a Negro named Buford Munson, who had come to get a jug filled, had to finish it and drag the body from the breakfast table where it was still sitting and bury it in a decent and Christian way, with the sign of its Saviour at the head of the grave and enough dirt on top to keep the dogs from digging it up.

Flannery O'Connor's masterwork, *The Violent Bear It Away*, ends with the fourteen-year-old Tarwater marching towards the city of destruction, where his own career as prophet is to be suffered:

> Intermittently the boy's jagged shadow slanted across the road ahead of him as if it cleared a rough path toward his goal. His singed eyes, black in their deep sockets, seemed already to envision the fate that awaited him but he moved steadily on, his face set toward the dark city, where the children of God lay sleeping.

In Flannery O'Connor's fierce vision, the children of God, all of us, always are asleep in the outward life. Young Tarwater, clearly O'Connor's surrogate, is in clinical terms a borderline schizophrenic, subject to auditory hallucinations in which he hears the advice of an imaginary friend who is overtly the Christian Devil. But clinical terms are utterly alien to O'Connor, who accepts only theological namings and unnamings. This is necessarily a spiritual strength in

1

O'Connor, yet it can be an aesthetic distraction also, since *The Violent Bear It Away* is a fiction of preternatural power, and not a religious tract. Rayber, the antagonist of both prophets, old and young Tarwater, is an aesthetic disaster, whose defects in representation alone keep the book from making a strong third with Faulkner's *As I Lay Dying* and Nathanael West's *Miss Lonelyhearts*. O'Connor despises Rayber, and cannot bother to make him even minimally persuasive. We wince at his unlikely verbal mixture of popular sociology and confused psychology, as even Sally Fitzgerald, O'Connor's partisan, is compelled to admit:

> Her weaknesses — a lack of perfect familiarity with the terminology
> of the secular sociologists, psychologists, and rationalists she often
> casts as adversary figures, and an evident weighting of the scales
> against them all — are present in the character of Rayber (who com-
> bines all three categories).

One hardly believes that a perfect familiarity with the writings say of David Riesman, Erik Erikson, and Karl Popper would have enabled O'Connor to make poor Rayber a more plausible caricature of what she despised. We remember *The Violent Bear It Away* for its two prophets, and particularly young Tarwater, who might be called a Gnostic version of Huckleberry Finn. What makes us free is the Gnosis, according to the most ancient of heresies. O'Connor, who insisted upon her Catholic orthodoxy, necessarily believed that what makes us free is baptism in Christ, and for her the title of her novel was its most important aspect, since the words are spoken by Jesus himself:

> But what went ye out for to see? A prophet? yea, I say unto you, and
> more than a prophet.
>   For this is *he,* of whom it is written, Behold, I send my messenger
> before thy face, which shall prepare thy way before thee.
>   Verily I say unto you, Among them that are born of women there
> hath not risen a greater than John the Baptist: notwithstanding he
> that is least in the kingdom of heaven is greater than he.
>   And from the days of John the Baptist until now the kingdom of
> heaven suffereth violence, and the violent take it by force.

I have quoted the King James Version of Matt. 11:9–12, where "and the violent take it by force" is a touch more revealing than O'Connor's Catholic version, "and the violent bear it away." For O'Connor, we are back in or rather never have left Christ's time of urgency, and her heart is with those like the Tarwaters who know that the kingdom of heaven will suffer them to take it by force:

> The lack of realism would be crucial if this were a realistic novel or if
> the novel demanded the kind of realism you demand. I don't believe

it does. The old man is very obviously not a Southern Baptist, but an independent, a prophet in the true sense. The true prophet is inspired by the Holy Ghost, not necessarily by the dominant religion of his region. Further, the traditional Protestant bodies of the South are evaporating into secularism and respectability and are being replaced on the grass roots level by all sorts of strange sects that bear not much resemblance to traditional Protestantism—Jehovah's Witnesses, snake-handlers, Free Thinking Christians, Independent Prophets, the swindlers, the mad, and sometimes the genuinely inspired. A character has to be true to his own nature and I think the old man is that. He was a prophet, not a church-member. As a prophet, he has to be a natural Catholic. Hawthorne said he didn't write novels, he wrote romances; I am one of his descendants.

O'Connor's only disputable remark in this splendid defense of her book is the naming of old Tarwater as "a natural Catholic." Hawthorne's descendant she certainly was, by way of Faulkner, T. S. Eliot, and Nathanael West, but though Hawthorne would have approved her mode, he would have been shocked by her matter. To ignore what is authentically shocking about O'Connor is to misread her weakly. It is not her incessant violence that is troublesome but rather her passionate endorsement of that violence as the only way to startle her secular readers into a spiritual awareness. As a visionary writer, she is determined to take us by force, to bear us away so that we may be open to the possibility of grace. Her unbelieving reader is represented by the grandmother in the famous story "A Good Man Is Hard to Find":

> She saw the man's face twisted close to her own as if he were going to cry and she murmured, "Why you're one of my babies. You're one of my own children!" She reached out and touched him on the shoulder. The Misfit sprang back as if a snake had bitten him and shot her three times through the chest. Then he put his gun down on the ground and took off his glasses and began to clean them.

That murmur of recognition is what matters for O'Connor. The Misfit speaks for her in his mordant observation: "She would of been a good woman, if it had been somebody there to shoot her every minute of her life." Secular critic as I am, I need to murmur: "Surely that does make goodness a touch too strenuous?" But O'Connor anticipates our wounded outcries of nature against grace, since we understandably prefer a vision that corrects nature without abolishing it. Young Tarwater himself, as finely recalcitrant a youth as Huckleberry Finn, resists not only Rayber but the tuition of old Tarwater. A kind of swamp fox, like the Revolutionary hero for whom he was named, the boy Tarwater waits for his own call, and accepts his own prophetic election only after he has baptized his idiot cousin Bishop by drowning him, and even then only in consequence of having suffered a homosexual rape by the Devil himself. O'Connor's audacity reminds us of the Faulkner of *Sanctuary* and the West of *A Cool Million*. Her theology purports to be Roman Catholicism, but her sensibility is Southern Gothic, Jacobean in the mode of the early T. S. Eliot, and even Gnostic, in the rough manner of Carlyle, a writer she is likely never to have read.

I myself find it a critical puzzle to read her two novels, *Wise Blood* and *The Violent Bear It Away*, and her two books of stories, *A Good Man Is Hard to Find* and *Everything That Rises Must Converge*, and then to turn from her fiction to her occasional prose in *Mystery and Manners*, and her letters in *The Habit of Being*. The essayist and letter-writer denounces Manichaeism, Jansenism, and all other deviations from normative Roman Catholicism, while the storyteller seems a curious blend of the ideologies of Simone Weil reading the New Testament into the *Iliad*'s "poem of force" and of René Girard assuring us that there can be no return of the sacred without violence. Yet the actual O'Connor, in her letters, found Weil "comic and terrible," portraying the perpetual waiter for grace as an "angular intellectual proud woman approaching God inch by inch with ground teeth," and I suspect she would have been as funny about the violent thematicism of Girard.

To find something of a gap between O'Connor as lay theologue and O'Connor as a storyteller verging upon greatness may or may not be accurate but in any case intends to undervalue neither the belief nor the fiction. I suspect though that the fiction's implicit theology is very different from what O'Connor thought it to be, a difference that actually enhances the power of the novels and stories. It is not accidental that *As I Lay Dying* and *Miss Lonelyhearts* were the only works of fiction that O'Connor urged upon Robert Fitzgerald, or that her own prose cadences were haunted always by the earlier rather than the later Eliot. *The Waste Land, As I Lay Dying*, and *Miss Lonelyhearts* are not works of the Catholic imagination but rather of that Gnostic pattern Gershom Scholem termed "redemption through sin." *Wise Blood, The Violent Bear It Away*, and stories like "A Good Man Is Hard to Find" and the merciless "Parker's Back," take place in the same cosmos as *The Waste Land, As I Lay Dying*, and *Miss Lonelyhearts*. This world is the American version of the cosmological emptiness that the ancient Gnostics called the *kenoma*, a sphere ruled by a demiurge who has usurped the alien God, and who has exiled God out of history and beyond the reach of our prayers.

II

In recognizing O'Connor's fictive universe as being essentially Gnostic, I dissent not only from her own repudiation of heresy but from the sensitive reading of Jefferson Humphries, who links O'Connor to Proust in an "aesthetic of violence":

> For O'Connor, man has been his own demiurge, the author of his own fall, the keeper of his own cell. . . .
>
> The chief consequence of this partly willful, partly inherited alienation from the sacred is that the sacred can only intrude upon human perception as a violence, a rending of the fabric of daily life.

On this account, which remains normative, whether Hebraic or Catholic, we are fallen into the *kenoma* through our own culpability. In the Gnostic formulation, creation and fall were one and the same event, and all that can save us is a certain spark within us, a spark that is no part of the creation but rather goes back to the original abyss. The grandeur or sublimity that shines through the ruined creation is a kind of abyss-radiance, whether in Blake or Carlyle or the early Eliot or in such novelistic masters of the grotesque as Faulkner, West, and O'Connor.

The ugliest of O'Connor's stories, yet one of the strongest, is "A View of the Woods" in *Everything That Rises Must Converge*. Its central characters are the seventy-nine-year-old Mr. Fortune, and his nine-year-old granddaughter, Mary Fortune Pitts. I am uncertain which of the two is the more abominable moral character or hideous human personality, partly because they resemble one another so closely in selfishness, obduracy, false pride, sullenness, and just plain meanness. At the story's close, a physical battle between the two leaves the little girl a corpse, throttled and with her head smashed upon a rock, while her grandfather suffers a heart attack, during which he has his final "view of the woods," in one of O'Connor's typically devastating final paragraphs:

> Then he fell on his back and looked up helplessly along the bare trunks into the tops of the pines and his heart expanded once more with a convulsive motion. It expanded so fast that the old man felt as if he were being pulled after it through the woods, felt as if he were running as fast as he could with the ugly pines toward the lake. He perceived that there would be a little opening there, a little place where he could escape and leave the woods behind him. He could see it in the distance already, a little opening where the white sky was reflected in the water. It grew as he ran toward it until suddenly the whole lake opened up before him, riding majestically in little corrugated folds toward his feet. He realized suddenly that he could not swim and that he had not bought the boat. On both sides of him he saw that the gaunt trees had thickened into mysterious dark files that were marching across the water and away into the distance. He

looked around desperately for someone to help him but the place
was deserted except for one huge yellow monster which sat to the
side, as stationary as he was, gorging itself on clay.

The huge yellow monster is a bulldozer, and so is the dying Mr. Fortune,
and so was the dead Mary Fortune Pitts. What sustains our interest in such anti-
pathetic figures in so grossly unsympathetic a world? O'Connor's own commentary does not help answer the question, and introduces a bafflement quite its
own:

> The woods, if anything, are the Christ symbol. They walk across the
> water, they are bathed in a red light, and they in the end escape the
> old man's vision and march off over the hills. The name of the story
> is a view of the woods and the woods alone are pure enough to be a
> Christ symbol if anything is. Part of the tension of the story is
> created by Mary Fortune and the old man being images of each other
> but opposite in the end. One is saved and the other is dammed [sic]
> and there is no way out of it, it must be pointed out and underlined.
> Their fates are different. One has to die first because one kills the
> other, but you have read it wrong if you think they die in different
> places. The old man dies by her side; he only thinks he runs to the
> edge of the lake, that is his vision.

What divine morality it can be that saves Mary Fortune and damns her
wretched grandfather is beyond my ken, but the peculiarities of O'Connor's
sense of the four last things transcend me at all times, anyway. What is more interesting is O'Connor's own final view of the woods. Her sacramental vision
enables her to see Christ in "the gaunt trees [that] had thickened into
mysterious dark files that were marching across the water and away into the distance." Presumably their marching away is emblematic of Mr. Fortune's damnation, so far as O'Connor is concerned. As a reader of herself, I cannot rank
O'Connor very high here. Surely Mary Fortune is as damnable and damned as
her grandfather, and the woods are damnable and damned also. They resemble
not the normative Christ but the Jesus of the Gnostic texts, whose phantom only
suffers upon the cross while the true Christ laughs far off in the alien heavens, in
the ultimate abyss.

O'Connor's final visions are more equivocal than she evidently intended.
Here is the conclusion of "Revelation":

> Until the sun slipped finally behind the tree line, Mrs. Turpin re-
> mained there with her gaze bent to them as if she were absorbing
> some abysmal life-giving knowledge. At last she lifted her head.

There was only a purple streak in the sky, cutting through a field of crimson and leading, like an extension of the highway, into the descending dusk. She raised her hands from the side of the pen in a gesture hieratic and profound. A visionary light settled in her eyes. She saw the streak as a vast swinging bridge extending upward from the earth through a field of living fire. Upon it a vast horde of souls were rumbling toward heaven. There were whole companies of white-trash, clean for the first time in their lives, and bands of black niggers in white robes, and battalions of freaks and lunatics shouting and clapping and leaping like frogs. And bringing up the end of the procession was a tribe of people whom she recognized at once as those who, like herself and Claud, had always had a little of everything and the God-given wit to use it right. She leaned forward to observe them closer. They were marching behind the others with great dignity, accountable as they had always been for good order and common sense and respectable behavior. They alone were on key. Yet she could see by their shocked and altered faces that even their virtues were being burned away. She lowered her hands and gripped the rail of the hog pen, her eyes small but fixed unblinkingly on what lay ahead. In a moment the vision faded but she remained where she was, immobile.

At length she got down and turned off the faucet and made her slow way on the darkening path to the house. In the woods around her the invisible cricket choruses had struck up, but what she heard were the voices of the souls climbing upward into the starry field and shouting hallelujah.

This is meant to burn away false or apparent virtues, and yet consumes not less than everything. In O'Connor's mixed realm, which is neither nature nor grace, Southern reality nor private phantasmagoria, all are necessarily damned, not by an aesthetic of violence but by a Gnostic aesthetic in which there is no knowing unless the knower becomes one with the known. Her Catholic moralism masked from O'Connor something of her own aesthetic of the grotesque. Certainly her essay on "Some Aspects of the Grotesque in Southern Fiction" evades what is central in her own praxis:

Whenever I'm asked why Southern writers particularly have a penchant for writing about freaks, I say it is because we are still able to recognize one. To be able to recognize a freak, you have to have some conception of the whole man, and in the South the general conception of man is still, in the main, theological. That is a large statement, and it is dangerous to make it, for almost anything you say about Southern belief can be denied in the next breath with equal propriety. But approaching the subject from the standpoint of the writer, I think it is safe to say that while the South is hardly Christ-centered, it is most certainly Christ-haunted. The Southerner, who isn't convinced of it, is very much afraid that he may have been formed in the image and likeness of God. Ghosts can be very fierce and instructive. They cast strange shadows, particularly in our litera-ture. In any case, it is when the freak can be sensed as a figure for our essential displacement that he attains some depth in literature.

The freakish displacement here is from "wholeness," which is then des-cribed as the state of having been made in the image or likeness of God. But that mode, displacement, is not what is operative in O'Connor's fiction. Her own favorite, among her people, is young Tarwater, who is not a freak, and who is so likeable because he values his own freedom above everything and anyone, even his call as a prophet. We are moved by Tarwater because of his recalcitrance, because he is the Huck Finn of visionaries. But he moves O'Connor, even to identification, because of his inescapable prophetic vocation. It is the interplay between Tarwater fighting to be humanly free, and Tarwater besieged by his great-uncle's training, by the internalized Devil, and most of all by O'Connor's own ferocious religious zeal, that constitutes O'Connor's extraordinary artistry. Her pious admirers to the contrary, O'Connor would have bequeathed us even stronger novels and stories, of the eminence of Faulkner's, if she had been able to restrain her spiritual tendentiousness.

JOHN HAWKES

Flannery O'Connor's Devil

Eventually students of literature may come to think of Flannery O'Connor not only in terms of coldness, detachment and "black" humor but also in terms of an older or more familiar traditon. In a letter not long ago she said, "I think I would admit to writing what Hawthorne called 'romances'. . . . I feel more of a kinship with Hawthorne than with any other American writer. . . ." Surely such an expression of kinship is a sober one, coming as it does from a comic writer whose humor was described as "slam-bang" and whose style was called "as balefully direct as a death sentence" by *Time* magazine. But of course this comic writer is a serious writer—say, in her moral preoccupations, her poetic turn of mind and incredible uses of paradox—and her remark about her affinity with Hawthorne deserves juxtaposition, it seems to me, with a statement such as this one from Edwin Honig's book on allegory: "Melville's problem, like Hawthorne's, was to find a method whereby a vigorous moral and aesthetic authority could be recreated in fiction. For him, as for his predecessors, the challenge was to map out the relation of the unknown country of allegory to the known countries and conditions of contemporary actuality."

That this statement is more appropriate to Flannery O'Connor than to most other contemporary American writers; that the problem and challenge it describes are curiously hers; that the authority it describes is precisely what lies behind her "brutal" laughter; that "unknown country" and "actuality" are precisely what her fiction combines in a mercilessly pleasurable tension—all this is reason enough for making the juxtaposition above. And also reason enough for raising and perhaps evading the final question of the extent to which Flannery

From *Sewanee Review* 70, no. 3 (July–September 1962). © 1962 by the University of the South.

O'Connor's work should be considered allegorical. But here I must mention my faith in the occult nature of minor coincidence since it was Melville's grand-daughter, a lady I was once privileged to know in Cambridge, Massachusetts, who first urged me to read the fiction of Flannery O'Connor, and—further—since this experience occurred just at the time I had discovered the short novels of Nathanael West.

At that time—about ten years ago—the sudden confluence of West and Flannery O'Connor to me suggested twin guffawing peals of thunder (the figure is borrowed from "The Life You Save May Be Your Own") above a dead land-scape quite ready for new humor, new vision, new and more meaningful comic treatments of violence. Though he died in 1940, West is the one writer who, along with Flannery O'Connor, deserves singular attention as a rare American satirist. I would propose that West and Flannery O'Connor are very nearly alone today in their pure creation of "aesthetic authority," and would also propose, of course, that they are very nearly alone in their employment of the devil's voice as vehicle for their satire or for what we may call their true (or accurate) vision of our godless actuality. Their visions are different. And yet, as we might expect, these two comic writers are unique in sharing a kind of inverted attraction for the reality of our absurd condition.

We may think of satire as "centralizing a dominant ideal by means of irony and analogy," and also as a form which "demolishes man's image of himself as a rational creature." It may be that most generally in West's satiric fictions the "dominant ideal," never more than implied, is merely the serenity of dissolu-tion, or release from the pains of sexual struggle and from the dead-end of an impossible striving toward God, all of this brought to "pitch" (to use Faulkner's word) by the comedy of the sexual struggle itself. Though Flannery O'Connor's "dominant ideal" is likely to be as difficult to discover as West's, it is nonetheless an absolute of which she is perfectly aware. She writes: "I don't think you should write something as long as a novel around anything that is not of the gravest con-cern to you and everybody else and for me this is always the conflict between an attraction for the Holy and the disbelief in it that we breathe in with the air of the times." Obviously West would never have made such a statement, and the polarity of the religious positions of these two writers is borne out in their novels.

West's preoccupation with the "Christ business" begins as joke in *The Dream Life of Balso Snell,* reaches a partly confused and sentimental climax in *Miss Lonelyhearts,* and in *The Day of the Locust* finally dwindles to sporadic and surface satires on the freak Hollywood church as bad answer. Whereas Flannery O'Connor's first novel, *Wise Blood,* concerns a circuit preacher's grandson who is so violently opposed to Christ that in the end, after an immolation that in-volves self-blinding (among other things), he is last seen by his worldly landlady as "going backwards to Bethlehem"; and *The Violent Bear It Away,* her recent and more ambitious novel, describes the metamorphosis of a similar young Fundamentalist into a prophet who accepts his burden and turns "toward the dark city, where the children of God lay sleeping."

But if West wrote less effectively whenever he attempted to take into account the presence or absence of God, while Flannery O'Connor would not write at all without what she calls the "attraction for the Holy"; or if it appears that Flannery O'Connor is writing about the spirit (the absurdity of disbelief), while Nathanael West was writing about the dream (the painful absurdity of sexual desire), at least I would say that the "pitch" of their comic fictions is very nearly the same. Both writers are demolishing "man's image of himself as a rational creature" (Flannery O'Connor, for instance, in her wonderfully unsympathetic portrait of the ridiculous school teacher, Rayber, in *The Violent Bear It Away,* and West in his creation of total and hapless dementia in *The Day of the Locust*). And both writers are reversing their artistic sympathies, West committing himself to the creative pleasures of a destructive sexuality, Flannery O'Connor committing herself creatively to the antics of soulless characters who leer, or bicker, or stare at obscenities on walls, or maim each other on a brilliant but barren earth. And finally both writers—one a Roman Catholic, the other a man of no particular religious drive—are remarkably similar in their exploitation of the "demolishing" syntax of the devil. But then a good many readers would mistake Flannery O'Connor's belief in the Holy for its opposite, in the same way that many readers might be misled into thinking of Nathanael West as a Christian *manqué.* The point is that in the most vigorously moral of writers the actual creation of fiction seems often to depend on immoral impulse.

It is obvious that West's distortions (his incorrigible giving way to joke, or his use of cathected patterns of physical detail in the place of conventional plotting) are constructed for the sake of psychological truth as well as from the sheer necessity for liberation from a constraining realism. Furthermore, it is obvious that his distortions depend in no way on an outside "framed" body of orthodoxy for their "authority." Once imagined, his comic vision *is* in fact its own authority. However, it needs to be said that Flannery O'Connor's work is just as great a violation of probability and of anticipated, familiar "reality " as West's. In *Wise Blood* two policemen turn out to be sadistic versions of Tweedledum and Tweedledee; in *The Violent Bear It Away* the devil himself quite literally appears, wearing a cream-colored hat and lavender suit and carrying a whiskey bottle filled with blood in the glove compartment of his enormous car; or, in this same novel, there is the comic fanaticism of the old great-uncle who continues to sit for a whole morning bolt upright at the breakfast table where he "died before he got the first spoonful to his mouth." And it also needs to be said that such fictive distortions of Flannery O'Connor are just as independent as those of Nathanael West.

Surely if the elements of Flannery O'Connor's fiction could be referred point for point to the established principles of a known orthodoxy, then many of the imaginative beauties and tensions of her fiction would disappear. But this is not the case. The very revivalist or circuit-preacher Protestant world of her fiction, with its improbable combination of religious faith and eccentricity, accounts in large part for the way in which "unknown country" and "actuality" are held in severe balance in her work. And then there is the creative impulse itself, so unflagging and so unpredictable as to become, in a sense, "immoral." Hovering behind the fiction this impulse has about it the energy and unassailable paradox of the grandfather in *Wise Blood,* who was "a waspish old man who had ridden over three countries with Jesus hidden in his head like a stinger." Within her almost luridly bright pastoral world—usually created as meaningless or indifferent or corrupted—the characters of Flannery O'Connor are *judged,* victimized, made to appear only as absurd entities of the flesh. Or, sometimes, they are allowed to experience their moments of mystery. But the mysterious baptismal drowning of an idiot child (to take one central example from *The Violent Bear It Away*) is in certain ways quite similar to the call—"full of melancholy and weariness, yet marvelously sweet"—of a trapped quail about to be cut apart with a pair of tin shears and fried in a skillet (*The Day of the Locust*). In other words, and thinking of artistic commitment in conflict with "dominant ideal," the improbable yet fictionally true Hollywood landscape of West is very like the improbable yet fictionally true "Free Thinking" evangelistic landscape of Flannery O'Connor. There is no security, no answer, to be found in either of these horrifying and brightly imagined worlds.

I have spoken of the devil's voice as vehicle for satire, and of the devil's "demolishing" syntax; and have suggested that there is a relationship to be found between fictive "authority" and "immoral" author-impulse in the comic works of West and Flannery O'Connor. To me it is important to stress these generalities because both West and Flannery O'Connor write *about* the devil, or at least about diabolical figures (most obviously Shrike in *Miss Lonelyhearts* and Tarwater's Friend—who is a literal *heard* version of the devil—in *The Violent Bear It Away*), but seem also to reflect the verbal mannerisms and explosively reductive attitudes of such figures in their own "black" authorial stances. When I suggested to Flannery O'Connor some time ago that as writer she was on the devil's side she responded at once—and of course to disagree.

Despite the comparison made above between the baptismal drowning of the idiot child and the "marvelously sweet" call of the trapped quail, it is clear that there is, actually, a considerable difference between the experiences of mystery as created by West and by Flannery O'Connor. No matter his preoccupation with the darkness of life, West could never have taken seriously an idea of the devil (as he could not an idea of the Holy), while on the other hand Flannery O'Connor has phrased this aspect of her concern with typical and shocking clarity: "I want to be certain that the devil gets identified as the devil and not simply taken for this or that psychological tendency." A statement as matter-of-fact as this one, with its explicit acceptance of the devil's existence and explicit renunciation of all his works, does little to help my argument concerning her "true" fictional allegiance—the more so since Flannery O'Connor herself has pointed out the difference between her devil (Lucifer, a fallen angel) and the authorial-devil I have been speaking of (to her no more than a subjective creation and rather alien to her thinking). But there is an interesting distance between the directness of her statement and profundity of belief, and the shifting, even deceptive substance of what Flannery O'Connor, with disarming humor and understatement, has called her "one-cylinder syntax." My own feeling is that just as the creative process threatens the Holy throughout Flannery O'Connor's fiction by generating a paradoxical fusion of improbability and passion out of the Protestant "do-it-yourself" evangelism of the South, and thereby raises the pitch of apocalyptic experience when it finally appears; so too, throughout this fiction, the creative process transforms the writer's objective Catholic knowledge of the devil into an authorial attitude in itself in some measure diabolical. This is to say that in Flannery O'Connor's most familiar stories and novels the "disbelief . . . that we breathe in with the air of the times" emerges fully as two-sided or complex as "attraction for the Holy."

Two passages from *The Violent Bear It Away* will illustrate the shifting substance of Flannery O'Connor's language and authorial attitude. The action of this novel is centered about a legacy of two obligations left to the young protagonist, Tarwater, by the old man (and Prophet) who is his great-uncle and who is also the medium through which the course of Tarwater's life is determined. One obligation is to bury the old man when he dies (which Tarwater fails to do because of the persuasive voice of his new Friend, the devil), and another is to baptize little Bishop, the idiot child (which Tarwater does manage to do, but against his will, and then only by drowning the "dim-witted boy"). The first passage below appears early in the novel and concerns the argument between Tarwater and his Friend over the burial; the second appears toward the end of the novel and concerns the lake in which the baptism finally occurs (the dialogue in both passages occurs in Tarwater's head, hence the absence of quotation marks; italicizing is mine):

Oh I see, the stranger said. It ain't the Day of Judgment for him (the

old Prophet) you're worried about. It's the Day of Judgment for you.
    That's my bidnis, Tarwater said.
    I ain't buttin into your bidnis, the stranger said. It don't mean a
thing to me. *You're left by yourself in this empty place. Forever by
yourself in this empty place with just as much light as that dwarf sun
wants to let in. You don't mean a thing to a soul as far as I can see.*

The first sight that met his eyes when he (Tarwater) got out of the car
at the Cherokee Lodge was the little lake. It lay there, glass-like,
still, reflecting a crown of trees and an infinite overarching sky. *It
looked so unused that it might only the moment before have been
set down by four strapping angels for him to baptize the child in.* A
weakness working itself up from his knees, reached his stomach and
came upward and forced a tremor in his jaw. *Steady, his friend said,
everywhere you go you'll find water. It wasn't invented yesterday.*

The Violent Bear It Away actualizes the truth of the devil's sentiments —
Tarwater does not, in fact, "mean a thing to a soul" and lives only in the stalwart
nausea of his resistance to the Prophet's calling and in the ultimate grim pleasure
of his acceptance of that call. By the end of the novel we know that Tarwater will
be destroyed by "the children of God," or destroyed by our godless actuality.
    But surely in giving voice to his dry country-cadenced nihilism and in lay-
ing out the pure deflated truth of mere existence ("Forever by yourself in this
empty place"), the devil is speaking not only for himself but for the author. Of
course the devil is attempting to persuade Tarwater that he is exactly like everybody else in "this empty place," and is attempting to persuade Tarwater to *be*
himself and to *do* what he wants, since given the fact of mere existence there is
nothing else to be or do. While of course the author is dramatizing the opposite,
that Tarwater is *not* like everybody else and that he is destined to suffer the extremities of the pain involved in the conflict between the "mean" earth and symbolic waters. However, the devil takes obvious pleasure in going about his own
"bidnis" and the author takes a similar obvious pleasure in going about hers.
And there are numerous examples to indicate that the author's view of "everybody else" is exactly the same as her devil's view. (There is the young mother
"whose face was as broad and innocent as a cabbage" in "A Good Man Is Hard to
Find"; there is the old woman who "was about the size of a cedar fence post" in
"The Life You Save May Be Your Own"; or the mother who has two little boys
who stand with faces "like pans set on either side to catch the grins that over-
flowed from her" in *Wise Blood*.)
    In these last examples the creation of flat personality — each instance is a kind
of small muffled explosion — depends on the extreme absurdity of juxtaposing

the human and the inanimate, and I think that the fact of the reductive or diabolical value judgment is clear, though to be sure there are degrees of judgment
and degrees of sympathy, too, in the range of Flannery O'Connor's wonderfully
merciless creations of the human type. But even more clear perhaps, or at least
more important, is the basic principle or association that fills out the devil's
nihilism and defines the diabolical attitude that lies behind the reversal of artistic sympathy — that is, the "meanness"-pleasure principle. When Tarwater discovers what he takes to be his freedom — for him it is the license to do whatever
he wants, and it comes to him while he is trying to dig his great-uncle's
grave — his first thought is simply, "Could kill off all those chickens if I had a
mind to. . . ." And Flannery O'Connor appears to reveal her own understanding of earthly (and, I would say, artistic) pleasure when she writes that "Haze
(the protagonist of *Wise Blood*) knows what the choice is and the Misfit (the
extraordinary convict in 'A Good Man Is Hard to Find') knows what the choice is
— either throw away everything and follow Him or enjoy yourself by doing some
meanness to somebody, and in the end there's no real pleasure in life, not even
in meanness." I suspect that for many readers today such a principle or such a
cold paradox of stringent alternatives would prove merely accurate or baffling or
offensive. Yet here, I think, is the core of traditional satiric impulse, or the core
of what we may call contemporary "anti-realistic" impulse.

However, to return to the italicized portions of the two passages quoted
above the *The Violent Bear It Away,* and noticing the similarity between the
devil's country-cadences or constructions and the author's, we might well ask
how a reader baffled by the purity of the devil's attitude and intention is to react
to an author capable of tilting our expectations *negatively* toward the apocalyptic by confronting us suddenly with the incongruous vision of "four strapping
angels." Certainly this second passage about the lake is lovely and shocking
both. We admire it essentially for the extreme compression within which the
writer modulates through three distinct "voices." That is, we are taken abruptly
but skillfully from the direct and unbiased allusion to spirituality (the "*crown* of
trees" and "infinite overarching sky") to the dispersive ambiguity of "unused"
(the word has the disturbing connotations of "unused" in the earthly pragmatic
sense — say, unused for boating — and hence extends this comically "realistic"
view of life into the other world — "unused" for baptism) to the thoroughly
double-purposed "angels" and Tarwater's sickness of recoil and anticipation,
and finally to the ultimate reduction of the devil's own absurdly pragmatic (and
at the same time pathetic) view of "invented" water. Here the shifting voices and
attitudes alone produce considerable tension. And even the devil's comic relief
— at once poised on the edge of incredibility but also actualizing simultaneously
the range of our possible "resistance" and the sheer fact of the impossibility of
resistance (even the devil knows the implication of "everywhere you go you'll

find water")—is in a sense an unwanted comic relief. However, the center of the tension for the reader, himself ensnared in the meanness-pleasure paradox, still lies in the metaphor of the "four strapping angels." If we consider what the passage might have been like had "four" and "strapping" been omitted ("It looked so unused that it might only the moment before have been set down by angels for him to baptize the child in") we become aware, first of the enormous loss that would have resulted from such omission, and second that the basis for the figure as it stands is a *literalness* which in its faithfulness to rationality is at once appropriate and absurd. Since literalness is also the basis of Fundamentalism, we may say that the figure returns us to the two components (improbability and "attraction for the Holy") originally seen as constituting the apocalyptic half of Flannery O'Connor's fiction. Or we may say that through her exploitation of satiric and sympathetic impulses she is attempting to maintain the balance of that conflict grounded in the fictional possibility of redemption. But my own feeling is that the comic humanizing of the giant "strapping" angels cannot be explained away in this fashion, and that it actually represents those creative impulses of the writer which point toward the other side of her imagination—the demonic.

I would not say that Flannery O'Connor's uses of image and symbol are inconsistent, but rather—to pursue the lines of this argument—that they are mildly perverse. If the writer commits herself at least creatively to the voice and attitude of her imagined devil, or if her imagined devil is at least a partial heightening of her own creative voice and attitude, then we have only to compare "that dwarf sun" with the "crown of trees" in order to interpret the very strength of her authority as being in a way perverse. In Flannery O'Connor's fiction personified nature is often minimized (the devil's view of the sun, or this corresponding author-description from "The Life You Save May Be Your Own": "A fat yellow moon appeared in the branches of the fig tree as if it were going to roost there with the chickens"). Or it is made to assume a baldly leering attitude toward the jocular evil antics of the men in its midst (the "guffawing peal of thunder" from the same story). And if Bishop, the little idiot child, is intended to establish an innocence that points towad the apocalyptic, old Singleton, an insane comic figure in "The Partridge Festival," is intended to be exactly the opposite—crazy and lecherous and pointing toward the demonic. The danger inherent in any oversimplified effort to discover consistent patterns or systems of traditional symbolic materials in this fiction is obvious (thinking of idiocy or insanity as traditionally sanctified conditions) when all at once the windshield wipers of an automobile make "a great clatter like two idiots clapping in church" (*Wise Blood*).

Certainly Flannery O'Connor reveals what can only be called brilliant creative perversity when she brings to life a denuded *actuality* and writes about a "cat-faced baby" or a confidence man with "an honest look that fitted into his face like a set of false teeth" or an automobile horn that makes "a sound like a goat's laugh cut off with a buzz saw." This much, I should think, is happily on the side of the devil.

Since I have mentioned that Flannery O'Connor does not agree with my notion of her central fictional allegiance, it is only right to say that our disagreement may not be so extensive after all, and that she has written that, "Those moments (involving awareness of the Holy) are prepared for — by me anyway — by the intensity of the evil circumstances." She also writes, "I suppose the devil teaches most of the lessons that lead to self-knowledge." And further that "her" devil is the one who goes about "piercing pretensions, not the devil who goes about seeking whom he may devour." If Flannery O'Connor were asked where she would locate the center of her creative impulse, she might reply, "in the indication of Grace." But then again she might not. And I suspect that she would not reply at all to such a question. It may be, too, that I have been giving undue stress to the darker side of her imaginative constructions, and that the devil I have been speaking of is only a metaphor, a way of referring to a temperament strong enough and sympathetic enough to sustain the work of piercing pretension. To think so, of course, takes much of the pleasure out of the piercing.

I shall continue to evade the final question of whether Flannery O'Connor is a writer of allegories, and whether she is to be associated with Hawthorne because he wrote "romances" or because he had his own indebtedness to evil principle. Very likely the principle and the form are inseparable. At any rate, and though the landscape is not as dead or mirthless as it was ten years ago, Flannery O'Connor's writing stands out against all those immediate fictions which are precious or flatulent or tending to retreat into the security of a constraining realism. The voice of her devil speaks with a new and essential shrewdness about what Nathanael West called "the truly monstrous."

ROBERT FITZGERALD

The Countryside
and the True Country

In this article I will be doing, or trying to do, something very limited. A full critical study of Flannery O'Connor's work remains to be done, and it will still remain to be done when I have finished. All I propose is to give a reading of one short story. One reason for my choice is that I believe it to be an important story and well achieved. Another reason is that a contrary opinion in a book review has been lodged for a long time in my copy of the book, and I'd like to dislodge it, so to speak. The review, of Miss O'Conor's collection called *A Good Man is Hard to Find,* appeared in *Time* for June 6, 1955. The impact of Miss O'Connor's writing had not been entirely lost on the reviewer. But this is what he had to say of the story in question:

"Only in her longest story, "The Displaced Person," does Ferocious Flannery weaken her wallop by groping about for a symbolic second-story meaning —in this case, something about salvation. But despite such arty fumbling, which also marred Author O'Connor's novel *Wise Blood* (*Time,* June 9, 1952), this is still a powerful and moving tale of an innocent Pole who stumbles against the South's color bar."

Let me look with care into this judgment and see first if I understand it. I would rather not take a high tone about it. The alliterations at the beginning, for example, would not be missed in good plain prose, but the reviewer probably did not have time for that. He did not have space for it, either. He wanted to make a reservation, pretty seriously, in the brief paragraph at his disposal. I wonder how, if at all, this reservation could be expressed more at length and in a lower key.

From *Sewanee Review* 70, no. 3 (July–September 1962). © 1962 by the University of the South.

There is difficulty for me right away in the notion of "groping." I can imagine a story itself seeming to grope; there are good stories that sometimes do. But the reviewer does not say this of Miss O'Connor's story. He says it of the writer, and there is something about the story which makes him say it. What it is about the story, I think, is that its meaning is unclear to the reviewer. He is aware of a meaning that eludes him, and perhaps because it eludes him he has hard words for it: it is "symbolic" and "second-story" and "something about salvation." Apparently he has done some groping of his own, as we might properly expect him to do, without being able to lay his hand on what he wanted. He blames this failure on the writer. He speaks as though the groping were all hers. My sympathy for the reviewer undergoes a strain when I see that all he has to show for his own groping, all he can offer as a hint of the meaning he cannot grasp, is the phrase "something about salvation." This comes from the blurb, which declares that "The Displaced Person" is "about the problem of salvation." A book reviewer should improve on blurbs or leave them alone.

Our reviewer adds one more hard word about the groping by calling it "arty fumbling." I associate the word "arty" with painted screens, but I know that this only dates me. A more recent fashion is referred to here, and I would like to define it fairly. I gather from the context that it must be a tendency derivable from modern literary studies, from the Age of Criticism if you will, to give the *dramatis personae* of a story representative weight as "symbols" or "archetypes." There is nothing new in this if you remember Aeneas, but no doubt Jane Austen was less interested in it than Thomas Mann. I would agree that as a fashion it can be distracting. The first, last, and best criterion for the worth of a work of fiction is probably James's: the amount of felt life that it contains. On the other hand, there is no denying representative value to figures in a story if in fact they have it, if they come by it honestly. Other things being equal, surely the more meaning a fiction has the better, or else Aristotle was wrong and history — and journalism — are superior to mimetic art.

As nearly as I can make it out now, our reviewer's reservation goes like this: "The Displaced Person" would be all right, or first rate, if one were not aware in reading it that its personages and action bear a meaning that one does not understand. If one has tried in vain to comprehend this meaning, that indicates that the writer has tried in vain to foist it on her story, being in this a slave to literary fashion. Too bad, because even though weakened by waste motion and the *trop voulu* it is still a powerful and moving tale.

The judgment, if I am right and that is it, would impress me more, or depress me less, if there were evidence that the reviewer had really gone to much trouble in making it. But I have already remarked how he resorted to the blurb for his shot at the intended meaning of the story. And that is not all. He also gives us a brief account of the subject and action: "an innocent Pole who stumbles against the South's color bar." You never can tell, of course, whose hand is responsible for any given sentence in *Time*. This one could have been written by an editor impatient to condense his book reviewer's painstaking distinctions. In any case, the brevity was a great mistake. Let me look at the story.

II

It begins:

> The peacock was following Mrs. Shortley up the road to the hill where she meant to stand. Moving one behind the other, they looked like a complete procession. Her arms were folded and as she mounted the prominence she might have been the giant wife of the country-side, come out at some sign of danger to see what the trouble was. She stood on two tremendous legs, with the grand self-confidence of a mountain, and rose, up narrowing bulges of granite, to two icy blue points of light that pierced forward, surveying everything . . . The peacock stopped just behind her, his tail — glittering green-gold and blue in the sunlight — lifted just enough so that it would not touch the ground. It flowed out on either side like a floating train and his head on the long blue reed-like neck was drawn back as if his attention were fixed in the distance on something no one else could see.

Now, I can easily conceive a reader thinking the peacock just incidental decoration, though the peacock is mentioned first, and a vanishing point for the story's perspective is suggested by his gaze. An inattentive reader might overlook this, but even an inattentive reader would assume from the beginning that the protagonist of the story is going to be Mrs. Shortley, and in this he would be right. The protagonist will be that giant wife of the countryside first personified by Mrs. Shortley and later by her successor in the role. In the opening sentence the reader is informed of the giant wife's purpose: she meant to stand.

The danger to be measured is the arrival of a Polish D. P., Mr. Guizac, with his family, on the farm of Mrs. McIntyre, for whom Mrs. Shortley's husband works as a dairyman. The countryside is Deep South, and just to make the intrusion thoroughgoing it is an old Catholic priest who has arranged to place the Guizacs with Mrs. McIntyre. We are given several pages in which to relish this situation through Mrs. Shortley's view of it.

> The man had on khaki pants and a blue skirt. Suddenly, as Mrs. McIntyre held out her hand to him, he bobbed down from the waist

and kissed it. Mrs. Shortley jerked her own hand up toward her mouth and then after a second brought it down and rubbed it vigorously on her seat. If Mr. Shortley had tried to kiss her hand, Mrs. McIntyre would have knocked him into the middle of next week, but then Mr. Shortley wouldn't have kissed her hand anyway. He didn't have time to mess around.

That will do for what could be called the traditional American response to European ways. There have been other European ways, and other responses.

Mrs. Shortley recalled a newsreel she had seen once of a small room piled high with bodies of dead naked people all in a heap, their arms and legs tangled together, a head thrust in here, a head there, a foot, a knee, a part that should have been covered sticking out, a hand raised clutching nothing. Before you could realize that it was real and take it into your head, the picture changed and a hollow-sounding voice was saying, "Time marches on!" This was the kind of thing that was happening every day in Europe where they had not advanced as in this country. . . . If the Guizacs had come from where that kind of thing was done to them, who was to say they were not the kind that would also do it to others?

It is cool work, this writing, in which not one but several human abysses are skated over with an ironic flick, and all in Mrs. Shortley's mind. We need not be deceived by the bare idiom, the parsimony of rhetoric. Here is Yeats' "uncontrollable mystery on the bestial floor." And these intimations of the abysmal, like the previous hint of a horizon beyond the actors' vision, should warn us that the story is religious. Other indications are soon to follow. By allusion and figure the religious background grows, and the foreground is ever more explicit. Going forward to be introduced,

Mrs. Shortley looked at the priest and was reminded that these people did not have an advanced religion. There was no telling what all they believed since none of the foolishness had been reformed out of it.

The priest is admiring the peacock behind her.

"So beauti-ful," the priest said, "A tail full of suns," and he crept forward on tiptoe and looked down on the bird's back where the polished gold and green design began. The peacock stood still as if he had just come down from some sun-drenched height to be a vision for them all.

Peacock and priest may seem equally exotic of the scene, but the Negroes, Astor and Sulk, are as much a part of it as the mulberry tree behind which Mrs. Shortley finds them. There are several distinct kinds of pleasure in reading Flannery O'Connor, and I find one kind in her dialogues between Negroes and whites.

> The old man, Astor, raised himself. "We been watching," he said, as if this would be news to her. "Who they now?"
>
> "They come from over the water," Mrs. Shortley said with a wave of her arm. "They're what is called Displaced Persons."
>
> "Displaced Persons," he said. "Well now. I declare. What do that mean?"
>
> "It means they ain't where they were born at and there's nowhere for them to go—like if you was run out of here and wouldn't nobody have you."
>
> "It seem like they here, though," the old man said in a reflective voice. "If they here, they somewhere."
>
> "Sho is," the other agreed. "They here."
>
> The illogic of Negro-thinking always irked Mrs. Shortley. "They ain't where they belong to be at," she said.

I have quoted this not only for itself but to show how deliberately the story goes and how close to the skin it is in local detail. It will continue to be leisured and joyously exact as the wife of the countryside, standing embattled, becomes an exponent of the countryside's religion. The intrusion of the D. P.'s kindles Mrs. Shortley's inner life to great intensity.

> Then she stood a while longer, reflecting, her unseeing eyes directly in front of the peacock's tail. He had jumped into the tree and his tail hung in front of her, full of fierce planets with eyes that were each ringed in green and set against a sun that was gold in one second's light and salmon-colored in the next. She might have been looking at a map of the universe but she didn't notice it any more than she did the spots of sky that cracked the dull green of the tree. She was having an inner vision instead. She was seeing the ten million billion of them pushing their way into new places over here and herself, a giant angel with wings as wide as a house, telling the Negroes that they would have to find another place.

In three weeks the Pole, who is expert, industrious and clean, has made such an impression on Mrs. McIntyre that she remarks to Mrs. Shortley, "That man is my salvation."

Mrs. Shortley looked straight ahead as if her vision penetrated the
cane and the hill had pierced through to the other side. "I would
suspicion salvation got from the devil," she said in a slow detached
way.

"Now what do you mean by that?" Mrs. McIntyre asked, looking
at her sharply.

Mrs. Shortley wagged her head but would not say anything else.
The fact was she had nothing else to say, for this intuition had only
at that instant come to her. She had never given much thought to
the devil for she felt that religion was essential for those people who
didn't have the brains to avoid evil without it. For people like
herself, for people of gumption, it was a social occasion providing
the opportunity to sing; but if she had ever given it much thought,
she would have considered the devil the head of it and God the
hanger-on. With the coming of these displaced people, she was obliged to give new thought to a good many things.

Several further revelations come to Mrs. Shortley before the last and most
enlightening. She perceives that the Negroes are not the only ones who may
have to find another place. Her husband's job is also in danger, especially if the
vigilant Pole should discover that he is running a still on the side. It occurs to her
that the priest, who is trying to convert Mrs. McIntyre, hopes to bring still
another Polish family to the place. Then she finds out something about the Pole
that would floor Mrs. McIntyre, but before she can use it two things happen.
The first is a vision.

Suddenly while she watched the sky folded back in two pieces like
the curtain to a stage and a gigantic figure stood facing her. It was
the color of the sun in the early afternoon, white-gold. It was of no
definite shape but there were fiery wheels with fierce dark eyes in
them, spinning rapidly all around it. She was not able to tell if the
figure was going forward or backward because its magnificence was
so great. She shut her eyes in order to look at it and it turned blood-
red and the wheels turned white. A voice, very resonant, said the
one word, "Prophesy!"

She stood there, tottering slightly but still upright, her eyes shut
tight and her fists clenched and her straw sun hat low on her forehead. "The children of wicked nations will be butchered," she said
in a loud voice. "Legs where arms should be, foot to face, ear in the
palm of hand. Who will remain whole? Who will remain whole?
Who?"

Just after this she overhears Mrs. McIntyre telling the priest that she is going to give Mr. Shortley notice. Mrs. Shortley has not been described as a giantess for nothing. Flaming with pride, she makes her husband help her to pack with fury all night, and loading their old car they decamp with their two girls before milking time in the morning. Only when they are on the dark road does he ask for the first time where they are going. At this, Mrs. Shortley's final revelation begins, coinciding with the heart attack that kills her.

> The two girls, who didn't know what had happened to her, began to say, "Where we goin, Ma? Where we goin?" They thought she was playing a joke and that their father, staring straight ahead at her, was imitating a dead man. They didn't know that she had had a great experience or ever been displaced in the world from all that belonged to her. They were frightened by the grey slick road before them and kept repeating in higher and higher voices, "Where we goin, Ma? Where we goin?" while their mother, her huge body rolled back still against the seat and her eyes like blue-painted glass, seemed to contemplate for the first time the tremendous frontiers of her true country.

III

That is Part I of "The Displaced Person." What is potential in the situation has been realized only in part: the ironic displacement of Mrs. Shortley, in a physical and then in a metaphysical sense. Along with a lot of comedy (most of it I have reluctantly skipped) we have had frequent intimations that the action is to be understood in religious terms: Mrs. Shortley herself so understands it. Her religious terms, as they become explicit under stress, are those of the countryside. I see no groping or fumbling in the way they are rendered but rather a widening of focus, at high velocity, from simple fear of the wicked nations to an apocalyptic inner light. Miss O'Connor's insight into what is left of Christianity in backcountry Bible-reading sections is profoundly empathic and satiric at the same time. Mrs. Shortley belongs to a great company of O'Connor revivalists and visionaries who are funny but by no means figures of fun. A page of prophecy in the Old Testament is hardly more eloquent than some of them, and I can think of nothing in literature that teaches better than they do why the Old Testament had to be completed by the New. Or, rather, why the whole Scripture overbrims all interpreters but one, the most capacious.

The mystery I have just mentioned certainly lies at the heart of this particular story. In most O'Connor stories we are aware of the Roman or universal

Church mainly by its absence. Here it is present from the start. I wonder if the handling of the peacock can justly be called arty. An unpredictable splendor, a map of the universe, doted upon by the priest, barely seen by everyone else: this is a metaphor, surely, for God's order and God's grace. Is it arbitrary and imposed? Can the reader be expected to see it? The *Time* reviewer did not, but then there is much that he did not see. What induced me to look at the story in detail was above all his brief account of protagonist and action: "an innocent Pole who stumbles against the South's color bar." Throughout Part I there is no doubt as to the chief actor; it is Mrs. Shortley. The Pole scarcely appears, his innocence or lack of it is neither here nor there, and the barrier he is up against has many bars besides the color bar. All this will be apparent to any fairly attentive reader. But it may be that few readers are prepared to understand the metaphor of the peacock, fewer still to approve. If our reviewer had understood it, he might still have called it arty, as a critic of another generation would have called it *recherché*. I can imagine him objecting that a peacock is a rare adornment on a Southern farm. To this I could only reply that that, in a way, is the point.

After Mrs. Shortley's death, her role as the giant wife of the countryside devolves upon Mrs. McIntyre, who being still more formidable will engage in a harder struggle. I have noted more than once how Mrs. Shortley became an exponent of the countryside's religion. Mrs. McIntyre does not know it, but she holds a later form of the same religion, so far reformed that no nonsense at all remains. It is a managerial religion, the one by which daily business in a realm gets done. This makes it still a little old-fashioned. If it were citified here, or professional or academic, Miss O'Connor on her record would parody it to put life into it, for her talent is Pauline in abiding not the lukewarm. But Mrs. McIntyre has savor and is played straight. She is rendered in fact with as much economy and energy as Mrs. Shortley, for whom she properly feels a kinship; she, too, undoubtedly feels that religion is for people without enough gumption to avoid evil without it. I can't refrain from quoting this description of her husband, the late Judge:

> He was a dirty snuff-dipping Court House figure, famous all over the county for being rich, who wore high-top shoes, a string tie, a gray suit with a black stripe in it, and a yellowed panama hat, winter and summer. His teeth and hair were tobacco-colored and his face a clay pink pitted and tracked with mysterious prehistoric-looking marks as if he had been unearthed among fossils. There had been a peculiar odor about him of sweaty fondled bills but he never carried money on him or had a nickel to show.

The industrious D. P. had imperilled the Shortleys' position; for Mrs. McIntyre he soon appears to imperil the social order that she must govern, and on which she depends. Mrs. Shortley's discovery, now repeated by Mrs. McIntyre, is that the Pole has promised his sixteen-year-old cousin to the colored boy, Sulk, if Sulk will pay half the expense of bringing her from a refugee camp to America. As Sulk explains, "She don't care who she mah she so glad to get away from there." For Mrs. McIntyre, in her complacency over having found at last a really efficient hired man, the discovery is a terrible blow. Nothing the Pole could have done would have been more hopelessly wrong. Let me be a little insistent about this. It is not merely that he has stumbled against the color bar. It is the classic situation of tragedy in which each party to the conflict is both right and wrong and almost incomprehensible to the other.

> "Mr. Guizac," she said, beginning slowly and then speaking faster until she ended breathless in the middle of a word, "that nigger cannot have a white wife from Europe. You can't talk to a nigger that way. You'll excite him and besides it can't be done. Maybe it can be done in Poland but it can't be done here and you'll have to stop. It's all foolishness. That nigger don't have a grain of sense and you'll excite . . ."
>
> "She in camp three year," he said.
>
> "Your cousin," she said in a positive voice, "cannot come over here and marry one of my Negroes."
>
> "She six-ten year," he said. "From Poland. Mamma die, pappa die. She wait in camp. Three camp." He pulled a wallet from his pocket and fingered through it and took out another picture of the same girl, a few years older, dressed in something dark and shapeless. She was standing against a wall with a short woman who apparently had no teeth. "She mamma," he said pointing to the woman. "She die in two camp."
>
> "Mr. Guizac," Mrs. McIntyre said, pushing the picture back at him, "I will not have my niggers upset. I cannot run this place without my niggers. I can run it without you but not without them and if you mention this girl to Sulk again, you won't have a job with me. Do you understand?"

When the priest comes to see her again, Mrs. McIntyre cannot listen to his talk about Purgatory. She interrupts to tell him that if she can find a white man who understands her Negroes, Mr. Guizac will have to go. This is a bold little scene, concluding in a kind of fugue.

> He turned then and looked her in the face. "He has nowhere to go," he said. Then he said, "Dear lady, I know you well enough to know you wouldn't turn him out for a trifle!" and without waiting for an

answer, he raised his hand and gave her his blessing in a rumbling voice.

She smiled angrily and said, "I didn't create his situation, of course."

The priest let his eyes wander toward the birds. They had reached the middle of the lawn. The cock stopped suddenly and, curving his neck backward, he raised his tail and spread it with a shimmering timbrous noise. Tiers of small pregnant suns floated in a green-gold haze over his head. The priest stood transfixed, his jaw slack. Mrs. McIntyre wondered where she had ever seen such an idiotic old man. "Christ will come like that!" he said in a loud gay voice and wiped his hand over his mouth and stood there, gaping.

Mrs. McIntyre's face assumed a set puritanical expression and she reddened. Christ in the conversation embarrassed her the way sex had her mother. "It is not my responsibility that Mr. Guizac has nowhere to go," she said. "I don't find myself responsible for all the extra people in the world."

The old man didn't seem to hear her. His attention was fixed on the cock, who was taking minute steps backward, his head against the spread tail. "The Transfiguration," she murmured.

She had no idea what he was talking about. "Mr. Guizac didn't have to come here in the first place," she said, giving him a hard look.

The cock lowered his tail and began to pick grass.

"He didn't have to come in the first place," she repeated, emphasizing each word.

The old man smiled absently. "He came to redeem us," he said and blandly reached for her hand and shook it and said he must go.

The struggle that now works itself out in Mrs. McIntyre is an unequal one, as we see, but it is none the less prolonged. If I summarize baldly, let it be remembered that the story proceeds with no loss of particularity. Mrs. McIntyre does not in fact try to find another hired man. She doesn't have to; after a few weeks Mr. Shortley turns up again. In her relief she tells him she will give the Pole notice on the first of the month, but the day arrives and she does not do so. Before firing the Pole she wants to persuade the priest — who has been staying away — that she has no moral obligation to keep him. Meanwhile the sight of the D. P. moving quickly about the place becomes more and more irritating to her. When the priest returns, she is so wrought up that in the course of giving him all her arguments she tells him fiercely that as far as she is concerned, Christ was just another D. P. Mrs. McIntyre's inner life, like Mrs. Shortley's before her, has now become intense, and her expression of the countryside's religion more pointed. Still she delays. The first of the month comes again, and again she cannot act on the choice that she has made. There are sleepless nights, debates in dream. But now Mr. Shortley turns the town against her, and when this comes home to her she realizes that she has a moral obligation to get rid of the Pole.

As she approaches the toolshed for this purpose, Mr. Guizac is getting under the small tractor to repair it and Mr. Shortley is backing the large tractor out of the shed.

> He had headed it toward the small tractor but he braked it on a slight incline and jumped off and turned back toward the shed. Mrs. McIntyre was looking fixedly at Mr. Guizac's legs lying flat on the ground now. She heard the brake on the large tractor slip and, looking up, she saw it move forward, calculating its own path. Later she remembered that she had seen the Negro jump silently out of the way as if a spring in the earth had released him and that she had seen Mr. Shortley turn his head with incredible slowness and stare silently over his shoulder and that she had started to shout to the Displaced Person but that she had not. She had felt her eyes and Mr. Shortley's eyes and the Negro's eyes come together in one look that froze them in collusion forever, and she had heard the little noise the Pole made as the tractor wheel broke his backbone. The two men ran forward to help and she fainted.

IV

The catastrophe is of course Mrs. McIntyre's. Her hired helpers leave her, she must sell her cows, and she lives on, bedridden with "a nervous ailment." It is a powerful and moving tale, but it is not the tale of an innocent Pole nor except incidentally of the South's color bar. It is a tale of the displacement of persons, or better, of the human Person displaced. (When Mrs. McIntyre came to, she "felt she was in some foreign country where the people bent over the body were natives, and she watched like a stranger while the dead man was carried away in the ambulance.")

I should say that this has been Flannery O'Connor's essential subject. Her satire and irony, exuberance of ear and invention, are inseparable from the central knowledge that in varying degrees they serve. "Religious" is a poor word for this knowledge if it does not mean "knowledge of the world." She sees the South, it seems to me (who am no Southerner but no Northerner, either), as populated by displaced persons. Almost all her people are displaced and some are either aware of it or become so. But it is not a sectional or regional condition; it is a religious condition, common to North and South alike, common indeed to the world we live in.

The stories not only imply, they as good as state again and again, that estrangement from Christian plenitude is estrangement from the true country of man. Peacock and priest in this story are not really exotic; the fantasies of Mrs. Shortley are, and so is the self-sufficient pragmatism of Mrs. McIntyre. The story goes beyond most in exploring the reformed religion. Clearheaded and hard beset, Mrs. McIntyre embodies the giant wife of our countryside more effectively than Mrs. Shortley, and is the worthy protagonist of a tragic action. For, as I have said, her situation is tragic in the classic sense, and tragic in the commitment of will. Being what she is, she must reject not only the salvation offered, in terms of farm work, by the Pole, but that other salvation that she finds so exasperating to hear of from the priest. It is an ambitious and responsible work of fiction, and there is no fumbling about it.

ROBERT FITZGERALD

Everything That Rises Must Converge

The black sky was underpinned with long silver streaks that looked like scaffolding and depth on depth behind it were thousands of stars that all seemed to be moving very slowly as if they were about some vast construction work that involved the whole order of the universe and would take all time to complete. No one was paying any attention to the sky. The stores in Taulkinham stayed open on Thursday nights so that people could have an extra opportunity to see what was for sale.

Wise Blood

A catchword when Flannery O'Connor began to write was the German angst, and it seemed that Auden had hit it off in one of his titles as the "Age of Anxiety." The last word in attitudes was the Existentialist one, resting on the perception that beyond any immediate situation there is possibly nothing—nothing beyond, nothing behind, nada. Now, our country family in 1949 and 1950 believed on excellent grounds that beyond the immediate there was practically everything, like the stars over Taulkinham—the past, the future, and the Creator thereof. But the horror of recent human predicaments had not been lost on us. Flannery felt that an artist who was a Catholic should face all the truth down to the worst of it. If she worried about the side effects of the ungenteel imagination, she took heart that year from Mauriac's dictum about "purifying the source"—the creative spirit—rather than damming or diverting the stream.

In *Wise Blood* she did parody the Existentialist point of view, as Brainard

---

Cheney has said (in the *Sewanee Review* for Autumn, 1964), but the parody was very serious. In this and in most of her later writing she gave to the godless a force proportionate to the force it actually has: in episode after episode, as in the world, as in ourselves, it wins. We can all hear our disbelief, picked out of the air we breathe, when Hazel Motes says, "I'm going to preach there was no Fall because there was nothing to fall from and no Redemption because there was no Fall and no Judgment because there wasn't the first two. Nothing matters but that Jesus was a liar." And in whom is angst so dead that he never feels, as Haze puts it: "Where you came from is gone, where you thought you were going to never was there, and where you are is no good unless you can get away from it."

Note the velocity and rightness of these sentences. Many pages and a number of stories by this writer have the same perfection, and the novels have it in sections though they narrowly miss it as wholes. I am speaking now of merits achieved in the reader's interest: no unliving words, the realization of character by exquisitely chosen speech and interior speech and behavior, the action moving at the right speed so that no part of the situation is left out or blurred and the violent thing, though surprising, happens after due preparation, because it has to. Along with her gifts, patient toil and discipline brought about these merits, and a further question can be asked about that: Why? What was the standard to which the writer felt herself answerable? Well, in 1957 she said:

"The serious fiction writer will think that any story that can be entirely explained by the adequate motivation of the characters or by a believable imitation of a way of life or by a proper theology, will not be a large enough story for him to occupy himself with. This is not to say that he doesn't have to be concerned with adequate motivation or accurate reference or a right theology; he does; but he has to be concerned with them only because the meaning of his story does not begin except at a depth where these things have been exhausted. The fiction writer presents mystery through manners, grace through nature, but when he finishes, there always has to be left over that sense of Mystery which cannot be accounted for by any human formula."

This is an open and moving statement of a certain end for literary art. The end, and some of the terms used here, seem to me similar to those of another Christian writer who died recently, T. S. Eliot. I do not propose any confusion between a London man of letters who wrote verse and criticism and a Southern woman who wrote fiction, for indeed they lived a world apart. Only at the horizon, one might say, do the lines each pursued come together; but the horizon is an important level. It is also important that they were similarly moved toward serious art, being early and much possessed by death as a reality, a strong spiritual sensation, giving odd clarity to the appearances they saw through or saw beyond. In her case as in his, if anyone at first found the writing startling he could pertinently remind himself how startling it was going to be to lose his own body, that Ancient Classic. Sensibility in both produced a wariness of beautiful letters and, in the writing, a concision of effect.

When it comes to seeing the skull beneath the skin, we may remark that the heroes of both O'Connor novels are so perceived within the first few pages, and her published work begins and ends with coffin dreams. Her memento mori is no less authentic for being often hilarious, devastating to a secular world and all it cherishes. The O'Connor equivalent for Eliot's drowned Phoenician sailor ("Consider Phlebas, who was once handsome and tall as you") is a museum piece, the shrunken corpse that the idiot Enoch Emery in *Wise Blood* proposes as the new humanist Jesus.

> "See theter notice," Enoch said in a church whisper, pointing to a typewritten card at the man's foot, "it says he was once as tall as you or me. Some A-rabs did it to him in six months . . ."

And there is a classic exchange in "The Life You Save May Be Your Own":

> "Why listen, lady," said Mr. Shiftlet with a grin of delight, "the monks of old slept in their coffins."
> "They wasn't as advanced as we are," the old woman said.

The state of being as advanced as we are had been, of course, blasted to glory in *The Waste Land* before Flannery made her version, a translation, as it were, into American ("The Vacant Lot"). To take what used to be called low life and picture it as farcically empty, raging with energy, and at the same time, *sub specie aeternitatis*, full of meaning: this was the point of *Sweeney Agonistes* and the point of many pages of O'Connor. As for our monuments, those of a decent godless people, surely the asphalt road and the thousand lost golf balls are not a patch on images like that of the hillside covered with used car bodies, in *The Violent Bear It Away*:

> In the indistinct darkness, they seemed to be drowning into the ground, to be about half-submerged already. The city hung in front of them on the side of the mountain as if it were a larger part of the same pile, not yet buried so deep. The fire had gone out of it and it appeared settled into its unbreakable parts.

Death is not the only one of the last things present in the O'Connor stories; Judgment is there, too. On the pride of contemporary man, in particular on flying as his greatest achievement, Tarwater in *The Violent* has a prophet's opinion:

> "I wouldn't give you nothing for no airplane. A buzzard can fly."

Christ the tiger, a phrase in Eliot, is a force felt in O'Connor. So is the impulse to renounce the blessed face, and to renounce the voice. In her work we are

shown that vices are fathered by our heroism, virtues forced upon us by our im-
pudent crimes, and that neither fear nor courage saves us (we are saved by grace,
if at all, though courage may dispose us toward grace). Her best stories do the work
that Eliot wished his plays to do, raising anagogical meaning over literal action. He
may have felt this himself, for though he rarely read fiction I am told that a few
years before he died he read her stories and exclaimed in admiration at them.

The title of [*Everything That Rises Must Converge*] comes from Teilhard
de Chardin, whose works Flannery O'Connor had been reading at least since early 1961 when she recommended them to me. It is a title taken in full respect and
with profound and necessary irony. For Teilhard's vision of the "omega point"
virtually at the end of time, or at any rate of a time span rightly conceivable by
paleontologist or geologist alone, has appealed to people to whom it may seem
to offer one more path past the Crucifixion. That could be corrected by no sense
of life better than by O'Connor's. Quite as austere in its way as his, her vision
will hold us down to earth where the clashes of blind wills and the low dodges of
the heart permit any rising or convergence only at the cost of agony. At that cost,
yes, a little.

The better a poem or piece of fiction, the more corrective or indeed destructive it is likely to be of any fatuous happiness in abstractions. "Rising" and "convergence" in these stories, as the title story at once makes clear, are shown in
classes, generations, and colors. What each story has to say is what it shows. If we
are aware that the meaning of the stories is to be sought in the stories and well
apprehended in the stories alone, we may try a few rough and cautious statements about them. Thus the title story shows, amid much else in a particular action of particular persons, young and old and black and white to be practically
sealed off against one another, struggling but hardly upward or together in a
welter of petty feelings and cross purposes, resolved only slightly even by the
tragic blow. "Slightly," however, may mean a great deal in the economy of this
writer. The story is one of those, like "The Artificial Nigger" in her first collection and "Revelation" in this, in which the low-keyed and calibrated style is allowed a moment of elevation.

What is wrong in this story we feel to be diffused throughout the persons
and in the predicament itself, but in at least two of the stories, and those among
the latest and most elaborate, the malign is more concentrated in one personage. I
do not mean *il maligno,* as the Italians call the devil. There are few better repre-
sentations of the devil in fiction than Tarwater's friend, as overheard and finally
embodied in *The Violent;* but in these two stories, "The Comforts of Home"
and "The Lame Shall Enter first," the personage in question is not quite that.
He need not be, since the souls to be attacked are comparatively feeble. Brainless
and brainy depravity are enough, respectively, to bring down in ruin an irritable

academic and a self-regarding do-gooder. The latter story is clearly a second effort with the three figures of the novel, Tarwater, Rayber and Bishop, who are here reworked, more neatly in some respects, as Johnson, Shepard and Norton.

Other similarities link various stories to one another and to earlier stories. There is a family resemblance between Julian in the title story, Wesley in "Greenleaf," Ashbury in "The Enduring Chill" and Thomas in "The Comforts of Home." The Wellesley girl in "Revelation" is related to all these and to the girl in "Good Country People." In the various mothers of the stories there are facets of Mrs. McIntyre in "The Displaced Person." Parker in "Parker's Back" has some of the traits of a latter-day Hazel Motes. The critic will note these recurrent types and situations. He will note, too, that the setting remains the same, Southern and rural as he will say, and that large classes of contemporary experience, as of industry and war and office work and foreign travel, are barely touched if touched at all. But in saying how the stories are limited and how they are not, the sensitive critic will have a care. For one thing, it is evident that the writer deliberately and indeed indifferently, almost defiantly, restricted her horizontal range; a pasture scene and a fortress wall of pine woods reappear like a signature in story after story. The same is true of her social range and range of idiom. But these restrictions, like the very humility of her style, are all deceptive. The true range of the stories is vertical and Dantesque in what is taken in, in scale of implication. As to the style, there is also more to say.

She would be sardonic over the word *ascesis,* but it seems to me a good one for the peculiar discipline of the O'Connor style. How much has been refrained from, and how much else has been cut out and thrown away, in order that the bald narrative sentences should present just what they present and in just this order! What counts is the passion by which the stories were formed, the depth, as Virginia Woolf said of Milton, at which the options were taken. Beyond incidental phrasing and images, beauty lies in the strong invention and execution of the things, as in objects expertly forged or cast or stamped, with edges, not waxen and worn or softly moulded.

If we look for pleasure of a secondary kind such as we take in the shadings and suffusions of Henry James, I suggest that this is given in these stories by the comedy. There is quite a gamut of it, running from something very like cartooning to an irony dry and refined, especially in the treatment of the most serious matters. John Crowe Ransom was the first reader known to me to realize and say that Flannery O'Connor was one of our few tragic writers, a fact that we will not miss now in reading "The Displaced Person" in the first volume or "The Comforts of Home" in this. But it is far from the whole story. On the tragic scene, each time, the presence of her humor is like the presence of grace. Has not tragicomedy at least since Dante been the most Christian of *genres?*

I do not want to claim too much for these stories, or to imply that every story comes off equally well. That would be unfaithful to her own conscience and sense of fact. Let the good critic rejoice in the field for discrimination these stories offer him. Before I turn them over to him and to the reader, I should like to offer a reflection or two on the late masterpiece called "Revelation." One of its excellences is to present through a chance collection in a doctor's waiting room a picture of a whole "section" — realized, that is, in the human beings who compose it, each marvelously and irreducibly what he or she is. For one example of the rendering, which is faultless, consider this:

> A grotesque revolving shadow passed across the curtain behind her and was thrown palely on the opposite wall. Then a bicycle clattered down against the outside of the building. The door opened and a colored boy glided in with a tray from the drug store. It had two large red and white paper cups on it with tops on them. He was a tall, very black boy in discolored white pants and a green nylon shirt. He was chewing gum slowly, as if to music. He set the tray down in the office opening next to the fern and stuck his head through to look for the secretary. She was not in there. He rested his arms on the ledge and waited, his narrow bottom stuck out, swaying slowly to the left and right. He raised a hand over his head and scratched the base of his skull.

Not only do we see this boy for the rest of our lives; for an instant we hear him think. But the greater excellence of the story is to bring about a rising and a convergence, a movement of spirit in Ruby Turpin that is her rising to a terrible occasion, and a convergence between her and the violent agent of this change.

The terms of the struggle are intensely local, as they will be in all such struggles, but we need not be too shy about seeing through them to the meaning that lies beyond at the usual mysterious depth. How else but at a mysterious depth can we understand a pretty notion like the Soul of the South? What the struggle requires of Mrs. Turpin is courage and humility, that is clear enough. Perhaps as a reward for these, her eyes are opened. And the ascent that she sees at the end, in an astonishment like the astonishment of the new dead, takes place against that field of stars that moved beyond Taulkinham in *Wise Blood* and that hold for a small boy, in another of these stories, the lost presence of his mother.

LEWIS A. LAWSON

The Perfect Deformity: Wise Blood

If the content of *Wise Blood* seems bizarre and ludicrous, the rhetoric only reinforces that appearance. Extremely incongruous images, oxymorons, and synesthesia convince us that here indeed is a strange new world. Objects are like humans and animals, human beings are like animals and insects, and animals are like human beings. But the unconventional rhetoric is not an embellishment pasted upon a basically conventional view of the world. It is indeed a warped world, one which has been likened to a Chagall painting, and the comparison of the novel to the modern painting seems especially apt for Miss O'Connor often appears to share modern painting's preoccupations. Her world frequently is that of a dream (in keeping with her topsy-turvey aesthetic, dreams are perhaps the most lucid and conventional parts of the book), with characters who transpose themselves, with aimless action endlessly performed, with bizarre mixtures of the known and the unfamiliar. Surrealistically, soda fountain chairs are "brown toad stools," trees look "as if they had on ankle-socks," and a cloud has "curls and a beard" before it becomes a bird. The physical world partakes of the strangeness which colors character and action: the sky leaks and growls, the wind slashes around the house, "making a sound like sharp knives swirling in the air," and "the sky was like a piece of thin polished silver with a dark sour-looking sun in one corner of it."

Miss O'Connor believed that it was her Catholicism which prompted her to describe the world as a bizarre and sinister dream: "My own feeling is that writers who see by the light of their Christian faith will have, in these times, the sharpest eyes for the grotesque, for the perverse, and for the unacceptable." She further

From *Renascence: Essays on Values in Literature* 17, no. 2 (Spring 1965). © 1964 by Catholic Renascence Society, Inc. Originally entitled "Flannery O'Connor and the Grotesque: *Wise Blood*."

thought that such a specific vantage point suggested the themes with which she worked: "I will admit to certain preoccupations that I get, I suppose, because I'm a Catholic; preoccupations with belief and with death and grace and the devil." But while belief and grace offered spiritual incentive to her writing, death and the devil offered the human terrors which make fiction remarkable. "I'm born Catholic," she said, "and death has always been brother to my imagination. I can't imagine a story that doesn't properly end in it or in its foreshadowings." Her statement is borne out by the fact that *Wise Blood* begins and ends with a memento mori: "The outline of a skull under his skin was plain and insistent" and "The outline of a skull was plain under his skin and the deep burned eye sockets seem to lead into the dark tunnel where he had disappeared."

But, for all that has been said, there may linger a suspicion that content and form are not joined in *Wise Blood.* Nearly everyone who has commented on the novel has noticed the malformed characterizations, the complete absurdity of action and event, and other features which depart from convention. Is it not, then, a farfetched story, which the author has attempted to dignify by grafting on a highly unconventional rhetoric? I think not. Given the author's many statements of her intentions, we must assume that she would have expected her work to be judged by its communicability, and would not have departed from the conventional structure and treatment of the novel, if she had thought innovations in style or absurdities in content would detract from her vision.

I have suggested [elsewhere] elements of symbolism which seem to join content and form and which give qualities of coherency and unity to the work, but I believe that there is yet a motif to be traced which serves as a first ironic and later serious basis for the conception of Haze Motes, a motif which serves as a coagulant for the diverse aspects of the work. If one cannot create the perfect form perhaps the next best thing is to create the perfect deformity. Satirists have always chosen the latter course, and that seems to have been Miss O'Connor's choice. In her view, the only conflict that would sustain for her a work as long as a novel was that of belief versus disbelief. She could have, then, chosen to narrate the story of a modern saint. But such a story would have had the quality of sentimental and intrusive moralism, of preaching, about it which would have alienated the very audience which she wanted to reach. She could have, then, chosen to analyze the rather normal man's attempt to establish a meaningful spiritual relationship in a world where disbelief, especially in the guise of belief, is rampant. But the trouble with this approach would be that the character might be so like his audience that it would not have perceived his problem. That leaves, then, the opposite of the saint: the active disbeliever. Here a demonic figure could have been constructed, but a demonic figure would be without the desire to believe in the first place, and so there would have been no conflict. The ideal figure, it seems, would be a saint who disbelieved, that is, one who was actively searching for religious meaning (as opposed to the majority who passively accept the traditional view, although they secretly regard it as nonsense) but who did not find it in the established beliefs.

What would be better, then, than to posit the form first and then let the character grow to fit it? In this manner the possibility of ironical treatment is available at first, when the character differs completely from the form, when he does the right thing for the wrong reason. Then, as the character is inevitably forced into the form, it receives straightforward treatment; rather than work by opposites the author can then work by similarities, thus effecting the supreme irony: the only possibility of actively rejecting an idea to which the majority pays lip service is through the same behavior as that of actively accepting the idea, that is, both disbeliever and believer are "outsiders," in that they seriously think about their spiritual life, whereas most people are so immersed in a materialistic life that they neither accept nor reject religion.

The legend of St. Anthony could be the form. An Egyptian monk of the third century who was evidently a visionary, Anthony gave up his worldly property to go into the desert to live as an ascetic. Here the devil, often in the guise of animals, continually tempted him. The Temptation of St. Anthony early became an attractive subject for painters who wished to depict man in conflict with the demonic; painters from Martin Schoengauer to Salvadore Dali have utilized the legend. Nor have painters alone been fascinated by the possibilities of the legend; both Flaubert and Faulkner found it compelling.

Haze Motes at first seems an unlikely St. Anthony figure. But the wide differences in time and place become unimportant when the essentially similar natures of the two men are seen. Both are possessed with an overpowering sense of the importance of religious belief as the only force which can give order and meaning to their lives. And both use self-abasement to express their realization of the gulf which separates the human from the spiritual. One accepts a saint as a flagellant, but one is at first surprised that Haze Motes, the illiterate Tennesseean, unconsciously knows of the centuries-old method of chastising the flesh to purify the soul.

Once the suggestion is implanted that Haze is to be regarded seriously as a seeker after divine truth, rather than as just another Bible-beating Southerner, the departure from the form is begun. Whereas Anthony had renounced civilization to find God in the desert, it is in the desert that Haze finds his substitute for God; the army "sent him to another desert and forgot him again. He had all the time he could want to study his soul in and assure himself that it was not there." And where Anthony's confrontation with God had left him humble,

Haze's false truth goads him into pride; his actions at first betray his contemptuousness of other people, who may believe in the fiction that he has discarded, but soon his words reveal the prideful unbeliever: " 'I'm going to do some things I never have done before,' he said and gave her a sidelong glance and curled his mouth slightly."

Haze also departs from the form when he seeks the city; "God made the country but man made the town" is at least as old as St. Augustine, but for Miss O'Connor, who always conceives of the city as Sodom, such a moral geography is still valid. When Haze reaches the city, his life once again parallels St. Anthony's; according to the legend, St. Anthony was subjected to harassment by all sorts of demons, and the invention of all kinds of demonic forms became the distinguishing characteristic of paintings which used the Temptation as a subject. Haze, too, is bordered on all sides by monsters. With figure of speech, with description, and even with suggestive names—Hawks, Shoats—the author emphasizes that Haze has plunged himself into a chaos filled with every kind of monstrous apparition.

All of the characters have some animalistic aspect to their natures, and all represent some type of worldly threat to Haze's unworldly quest. Hawks is the fake preacher, unable at the moment of truth to act in the name of that which he had preached. Sabbath Lily Hawks is the complete sensualist, who recognizes that Haze is obsessed: "I knew when I first seen you you were mean and evil, . . . I seen you wouldn't let nobody have nothing. I seen you were mean enough to slam a baby against the wall. I seen you wouldn't never have no fun or let anybody else because you didn't want nothing but Jesus." And Hoover Shoats, who had posed as Onnie Jay Holy, is Haze's special tempter; like the pig which is generally shown in depictions of St. Anthony as a figure symbolic of sensuality and gluttony, the worst threats to his attempts to lead the religious life, Shoats is the particularly twentieth-century, bourgeois threat to Haze's religious vision; he sees the commercial possibilities of Haze's belief and he wants to make a confidence game of it: " 'Now I just want to give you folks a few reasons why you can trust this church—' "

Once the tension between the form, St. Anthony, and the departure from it, Haze Motes, has been established, there is little need for its constant emphasis. Rather, the novel is a series of events, or panels of a painting as it were, showing Haze being tormented by the symbolically different weird beasts. The motif is not reintroduced until near the end of the novel, when Haze has been forced to see that there is no escape from Christ. Structurally, of course, it is at this point when the departure from the form becomes the form. For the description of Haze's final, saintlike actions, the point of view is shifted to the eyes of Haze's horsey, lovesick landlady. After the destruction of his car, of his delusion,

Haze returns to blind himself. Thereafter his landlady, mainly because of his large disability check (which is one hundred per cent and suggests that Haze was a mentally exhausted victim of the war), takes great interest in Haze and observes him closely: "He could have been dead and get all he got out of life but the exercise. He might as well be one of them monks, she thought, he might as well be in a monkery." When she learns that Haze walks in shoes filled with rocks and broken glass and wears strands of barbed wire wrapped around his chest, she is convinced of his insanity: " 'Well, it's not normal. It's like one of them gory stories, it's something that people have quit doing — like boiling in oil or being a saint or walling up cats, . . .'"

Miss O'Connor was fully conscious that her work lay within a "school of the grotesque." She made several remarks about the presence of the grotesque in her art. Though she felt that modern life has made grotesques of us all, still, she thought that too often her work was termed "grotesque" when she had no intention of achieving that response. She justified her use of it as the only mode of illusion through which she could reach her audience. I doubt that she would have attempted a rigid definition for "grotesque"; she had used the term in too many contexts. I do believe, however, that her purpose in using it can be safely stated: the grotesque for her was a form of religious hyperbole. There is always the danger that an audience not attuned to the form will misunderstand such hyperbole. That is the chance that Miss O'Connor must have felt she had to take. Certainly she was deadly serious when she used the grotesque, and its use was not merely gratuitous. Just as certainly she was not merely celebrating southern degeneracy.

Flannery O'Connor was, on the contrary, perhaps the writer of the modern Southern school most conscious of the chaotic world caused by the declining belief in older religious institutions. Thus her satire was the most desperate, for to her it was most obvious that the old order was crumbling. But she saw that the old order in religion remained a husk; therefore she had to attack those people who play out their lives within the old form without giving allegiance to it and those people who have gone over more obviously to some other allegiance. There was no place in her world for any norms; from her vantage point the entire world did look grotesque, since her audience did not recognize the normative value of faith.

JOYCE CAROL OATES

The Visionary Art of Flannery O'Connor

Something is developing in the world by means of us, perhaps at our expense.
— TEILHARD DE CHARDIN

The greatest of Flannery O'Connor's books is her last, posthumously published collection of stories, *Everything That Rises Must Converge.* Though it is customary to interpret O'Connor's allusion to the philosophy of Teilhard de Chardin as ironic, it seems to me that there is no irony involved. There are many small ironies in these nine stories, certainly, and they are comic-grotesque and flamboyant and heartbreaking — but no ultimate irony is intended and the book is not a tragic one. It is a collection of revelations; like all revelations, it points to a dimension of experiential truth that lies outside the sphere of the questing, speculative mind, but which is nevertheless available to all.

The "psychic interpenetrability" of which Teilhard speaks in *The Phenomenon of Man* determines that man, in "rising" to a higher consciousness, will of necessity coalesce into a unity that is basically a phenomenon of mind (hence of man, since only man possesses self-consciousness). It is misleading to emphasize Teilhard's optimism at the expense of his cautious consideration of what he calls the "doctrine by isolation" and the "cynical and brutal theories" of the contemporary world; O'Connor has dramatized the tragic consequences of the locked-in ego in earlier fiction, but in *Everything That Rises Must Converge* nearly every story addresses itself to the problem of bringing to consciousness the latent

From *Southern Humanities Review* 7, no. 3 (Summer 1973). © 1973 by *Southern Humanities Review*, Auburn University, Auburn, Ala.

horror, making manifest the Dream of Reason — which is of course a nightmare. It is a measure of her genius that she can so easily and so skillfully evoke the spiritual while dealing in a very concrete, very secular world of fragmentary people.

Despite her rituals of baptism-by-violence, and her apparently merciless subjecting of ordinary "good" people to extraordinary fates, O'Connor sees the world as an incarnation of spirit; she has stated that the art of fiction itself is "very much an incarnational art." In a way she shares the burdens of her fanatical preachers Motes and Tarwater: she sees herself as writing from a prophetic vision, as a "realist of distances." Her people are not quite whole until violence makes them whole. They must suffer amazing initiation, revelations nearly as physically brutal as those in Kafka — one might explore the similarities between Parker of "Parker's Back" and the heroic, doomed officer of "In The Penal Colony" — because their way into the spiritual is through the physical; the way into O'Connor's dimension of the sacred is through the secular or vulgar. Teilhard's rising of consciousness into a mysterious Super-Life, in which the multiplicity of the world's fragments are driven to seek one another through love assumes a mystical "gravity of bodies" that must have appealed to O'Connor's sacramental imagination. Fundamental to the schoolteacher Rayber's insistence upon rationality is his quite justified terror of the Unconscious — he must act out of his thinking, calculating, mechanical ego simply in order to resist the gravity that threatens to carry him out of himself; otherwise, he will become another "fanatic," another victim of that love that is hidden in the blood, in this specific instance in terms of Christ. The local, human tragedy is, then, the highly conscious resisting of the Incarnation. As human beings (who are fragments) resist the gravity that should bring them into a unity, they emphasize their isolation, their helplessness, and can be delivered from the trance of Self only by violence.

Paradoxically, the way into O'Connor's vision that is least ambiguous is through a story that has not received much attention, "The Lame Shall Enter First." This fifty-seven-page story is a reworking of the nuclear fable of *The Violent Bear It Away* and, since O'Connor explored the tensions between the personalities of the Rationalist-Liberal and the object of his charity at such length in the novel, she is free to move swiftly and bluntly here. "We are accustomed to consider," says Teilhard in a discussion of the energies of love "Beyond the Collective," "only the sentimental face of love. . . ." In "The Lame Shall Enter First" it is this sentimental love that brings disaster to the would-be Savior, Sheppard. He is a young, white-haired City Recreational Director who, on Saturdays, works as a counselor at a boys' reformatory; since his wife's death he has moved out of their bedroom and lives an ascetic, repressed life, refusing even to fully acknowledge his love for his son. Befriending the crippled, exasperating Rufus Johnson, Sheppard further neglects his own son, Norton, and is forced to realize that his entire conception of himself has been hypocritical. O'Connor undergoes the religious nature of his experience by calling it a *revelation:* Sheppard hears his own voice "as if it were the voice of his accuser." Though he closes his eyes against the revelation, he cannot elude it:

> His heart contracted with a repulsion for himself so clear and so intense that he gasped for breath. He had stuffed his own emptiness with good works like a glutton. He had ignored his own child to feed his vision of himself. He saw the clear-eyed Devil, the sounder of hearts, leering at him. . . . His image of himself shrivelled until everything was black before him. He sat there paralyzed, aghast.

Sheppard then wakes from his trance and runs to his son, but, even as he hurries to the boy, he imagines Norton's face "transformed; the image of his salvation; all light," and the reader sees that even at this dramatic point Sheppard is deluded. It is still *his* salvation he desires, *his* experience of the transformation of his son's misery into joy. Therefore it is poetically just that his change of heart leads to nothing, to no joyous reconciliation. He rushes up to the boy's room and discovers that Norton has hanged himself.

The boy's soul has been "launched . . . into space"; like Bishop of *The Violent Bear It Away* he is a victim of the tensions between two ways of life, two warring visions. In the image of Christ there is something "mad" and "stinking" and catastrophic, at least in a secularized civilization; in the liberal, manipulative humanitarianism of the modern world there is that "clear-eyed Devil" that cuts through all bonds, all mystery, all "psychical convergence" that cannot be reduced to simplistic sociological formulas. It is innocence that is destroyed. The well-intentioned Savior, Sheppard, has acted only to fill his own vacuity; his failure as a true father results in his son's suicide.

He had stuffed his own emptiness with good works like a glutton.

Perhaps this is O'Connor's judgment, blunt and final, upon our civilization. Surely she is sympathetic with Teilhard's rejection of egoism, as the last desperate attempt of the world of matter—in its fragmentary forms, "individuals"—to persist in its own limited being. In discussing the evolutionary process of love, the rising-to-consciousness of individuals through love, Teilhard analyzes the motives for "the fervour and impotence" that accompany every egoistic solution of life:

> In trying to separate itself as much as possible from others, the element individualises itself; but in so doing it becomes retrograde and seeks to drag the world backwards toward plurality and into matter.

> In fact it diminishes itself and loses itself. . . . The peak of our-
> selves, the acme of our originality, is not our individuality but our
> person; and according to the evolutionary structure of the world, we
> can only find our person by uniting together.

What is difficult, perhaps, is to see how the humanitarian impulse — when it is
not spiritual — is an egoistic activity. O'Connor's imagination is like Dostoevsky's:
politically reactionary, but spiritually fierce, combative, revolutionary. If the
liberal, atheistic, man-centered society of modern times is dedicated to manip-
ulating others in order to "save" them, to transform them into flattering images
of their own egos, then there is no love involved — there is no true merging of
selves, but only a manipulative aggression. This kind of love is deadly, because it
believes itself to be selfless; it is the sudden joy of the intellectual Julian, in the
story "Everything That Rises Must Converge," when he sees that his mother is
about to be humiliated by a black woman who is wearing the same outrageously
ugly hat his mother has bought — "His grin hardened until it said to her as plain-
ly as if he were saying aloud: Your punishment exactly fits your pettiness. This
should teach you a permanent lesson." The lesson his mother gets, however, is
fatal: the permanence of death.

"He thinks he's Jesus Christ!" the club-footed juvenile delinquent, Rufus
Johnson, exclaims of Sheppard. He thinks he is divine, when in fact he is empty;
he tries to stuff himself with what he believes to be good works, in order to dis-
guise the terrifying face of his own emptiness. For O'Connor *this* is the gravest
sin. Her madmen, thieves, misfits, and murderers commit crimes of a secular
nature, against other men; they are not so sinful as the criminals who attempt to
usurp the role of the divine. In Kafka's words, "they . . . attempted to realize
the happiness of mankind without the aid of grace." It is an erecting of the
Tower of Babel upon the finite, earthly Wall of China: a ludicrous act of folly.

O'Connor's writing is stark and, for many readers, difficult to absorb into a
recognizable world, because it insists upon a brutal distinction between what
Augustine would call the City of Man and the City of God. One can reject
O'Connor's fierce insistence upon this separation — as I must admit I do — and
yet sympathize with the terror that must be experienced when these two "realms"
of being are imagined as distinct. For, given the essentially Manichean dualism
of the Secular and the Sacred, man is forced to choose between them: he cannot
comfortably live in both "cities." Yet his body, especially if it is a diseased and
obviously, immediately, *perpetually* mortal body, forces him to realize that he is
existing in that City of Man, at every instant that he is not so spiritually chaste as
to be in the City of God. Therefore life is a struggle; the natural, ordinary world
is either sacramental (and ceremonial) or profane (and vulgar). And it follows

from this that the diseased body is not only an affirmation, or a symbolic intensi-
fication of, the spiritual "disease" that attends physical processes; it becomes a
matter of one's personal salvation—Jung would use the term 'individuation'—to
interpret the accidents of the flesh in terms of the larger, unfathomable, but ultimately *no more abstract* pattern that links the Self to the Cosmos. This is a way
of saying that for Flannery O'Connor (as for Kafka and for D. H. Lawrence) the
betrayal of the body, its loss of normal health, must be seen as necessary; it must
make sense. *Wise Blood,* ironically begun before O'Connor suffered her first attack of the disease that ultimately killed her, a disease inherited from her father,
makes the point dramatically and lyrically that the "blood" is "wise." And rebellion is futile against it. Thus, the undulant fever suffered by the would-be
writer, Asbury, is not only directly and medically attributable to *his* rash behavior (drinking unpasteurized milk, against his mother's rules of the dairy) but it
becomes the means by which he realizes a revelation he would not otherwise
have experienced. Here, O'Connor affirms a far more primitive and far more
brutal sense of fate than Teilhard would affirm—at least as I understand Teilhard—for in the physical transformation of man into a higher consciousness and
finally into a collective, godlike "synthesized state" the transformation is experienced in terms of a space / time series of events, but is in fact (if it could be a
demonstrable or measurable "fact") one single event: one phenomenon. Therefore, the "physical" is not really a lower form of the spiritual but is experienced
as being lower, or earlier in evolution, and the fear of or contempt for the body
expressed by Augustine is simply a confusion. The physical *is* also spiritual; the
physical only seems not to be "spiritual." Though this sounds perplexing, it is
really a way of saying that Augustine (and perhaps O'Connor, who was very
much influenced by Augustine and other Catholic theologians) prematurely denied the sacredness of the body, as if it were a hindrance and not the only means
by which the spirit can attain its "salvation." Useless to rage against his body's
deterioration, Lawrence says sadly, and nobly, because that body was the only
means by which D. H. Lawrence could have appeared in the world. But this
is not at all what O'Connor does, for in her necessary and rather defiant acceptance of her inherited disease in terms of its being, perhaps, a kind of Original
Sin and therefore not an accident—somehow obscurely willed either by God
or by O'Connor herself (if we read "The Enduring Chill" as a metaphor for
O'Connor's predicament)—we are forced to affirm the disease-as-revelation:

> The boy [Asbury] fell back on his pillow and stared at the ceiling.
> His limbs that had been racked for so many weeks by fever and chill
> were numb now. The old life in him was exhausted. He awaited the
> coming of new. It was then that he felt the beginning of a chill, a

chill so peculiar, so light, that it was like a warm ripple across a
deeper sea of cold. . . . Asbury blanched and the last film of illusion was torn as if by a whirlwind from his eyes. He saw that for the
rest of his days, frail, racked, but enduring, he would live in the face
of a purifying terror. A feeble cry, a last impossible protest escaped
him. But the Holy Ghost, emblazoned in ice instead of fire, continued, implacable, to descend.

("The Enduring Chill")

This particular story and its epiphany may not have the aesthetic power to
move us that belong to O'Connor's more sharply imagined works, but it is central
to an understanding of all of her writing and, like Lawrence's "The Ship of
Death," it has a beauty and a terrible dignity that carry it beyond criticism. For
while Teilhard's monumental work stresses the uniqueness of the individual
through his absorption in a larger, and ultimately divine, "ultimate earth," there
cannot be in his work the dramatization of the real, living, bleeding, suffering, *existing* individual that O'Connor knows so well. She knows this existing individual
from the inside and not from the outside; she knows that while the historical and
sociological evolution causes one group of people to "rise" (the blacks; the haughty
black woman in "Everything That Rises Must Converge"), it is also going to
destroy others (both Julian and his mother, who evidently suffers a stroke when
the black woman hits her), and she also knows — it is this point, I believe, missed
by those critics who are forever stressing her 'irony' — that *the entire process is
divine*. Hence her superficially reactionary attitude toward the secularized, liberal,
Godless society, and her affirmation of the spontaneous, the irrational, the
wisdom of the blood in which, for her, Christ somehow is revealed. Because she
does believe and states clearly that her writing is an expression of her religious
commitment, and is itself a kind of divine distortion ("the kind that reveals, or
should reveal," as she remarks in the essay "Novelist and Believer"), the immediate problem for most critics is *how* to wrench her work away from her, *how* to
show that she didn't at all know herself, but must be subjected to a higher, wiser,
more objective consciousness in order to be understood. But the amazing thing
about O'Connor is that she seems to have known exactly what she was doing and
how she might best accomplish it. There is no ultimate irony in her work, no
ultimate despair or pessimism or tragedy, and certainly not a paradoxical sympathy for the devil. It is only when O'Connor is judged from a secular point of
view, or from a "rational" point of view, that she seems unreasonable — a little
mad — and must be chastely revised by the liberal imagination.

"Everything That Rises Must Converge" is a story in which someone appears
to lose, and to lose mightily; but the "loss" is fragmentary, a necessary and minor

part of the entire process of "converging" that is the entire universe — or God. The son, Julian, is then released to the same "entry into the world of guilt and sorrow" that is Rayber's, and Sheppard's, and his surrender to the emotions he has carefully refined into ironic, cynical, "rational" ideas is at the same time his death (as an enlightened Ego) and his birth (as a true adult). Many of the stories in this volume deal literally with the strained relationships between one generation and another, because this is a way of making explicit the psychological problem of ascending to a higher self. In *A Good Man Is Hard to Find* the tensions were mainly between strangers and in terms of very strange gods. The life you save *may* be your own, and if you cannot bear the realization that a freak is a Temple of the Holy Ghost, that is unfortunate for you. As Rufus Johnson says of the Bible, superbly and crazily, *Even if I didn't believe it, it would still be true* — a reply to infuriate the rationalist Sheppard, and no doubt most of us! But O'Connor's art is both an existential dramatization of what it means to suffer, and to suffer intelligently, coherently, and a deliberate series of parodies of that subjectivist philosophy loosely called "existentialism" — though it is the solipsistic, human-value-oriented existentialism she obviously despises, Sartrean and not Kierkegaardian. The Deist may say "Whatever is, is right," but the Deist cannot prove the truth of his statement, for such truths or revelations can only be experienced by an existing, suffering individual whom some violent shock has catapulted into the world of sorrow. When the intellectual Julian suffers the real loss of his mother, the real Julian emerges; his self-pitying depression vanishes at once; the faith he had somehow lost "in the midst of his martyrdom" is restored. So complex and so powerful a story cannot be reduced to any single meaning; but it is surely O'Connor's intention to show how the egoistic Julian is a spokesman for an entire civilization, and to demonstrate the way by which this civilization will — inevitably, horribly — be jolted out of its complacent, worldly cynicism. *By violence.* And by no other way, because the Ego cannot be destroyed except violently, it cannot be argued out of its egoism by words, by any logical argument, it cannot be instructed in anything except a physical manner. O'Connor would have felt a kinship with the officer of Kafka's "In the Penal Colony," who yearns for an enlightenment that can only come through his own body, through a sentence tattooed on his body. As Christ suffered with his real, literal body, so O'Connor's people must suffer in order to realize Christ in them.

Yet it is not finally necessary to share O'Connor's specific religious beliefs in order to appreciate her art. Though she would certainly refute me in saying this, the "Christ" experience itself may well be interpreted as a psychological event which is received by the individual according to his private expectations. No writer obsessively works and reworks a single theme that is without deep personal meaning, so it is quite likely that O'Connor experienced mystical "visions" or insights, which she interpreted according to her Catholicism; her imagination was visual and literal, and she is reported to have said of the Eucharist that if it were only a symbol, "I'd say the hell with it." This childlike or primitive rejection of a psychic event—*only* a symbol!—as if it were somehow less real than a physical event gives to O'Connor's writing that curious sense of blunt, graphic impatience, the either/or of fanaticism and genius, that makes it difficult for even her most sympathetic critics to relate her to the dimension of psychological realism explored by the traditional novel. Small obscenities or cruelties in the work of John Updike, for instance, have a power to upset us in a way that gross fantastic acts of violence in O'Connor do not, for we read O'Connor as a writer of parables and Updike as an interpreter of the way we actually live. Yet, because she is impatient with the City of Man except as it contrasts with the City of God, she can relate her localized horrors to a larger harmony that makes everything, however exaggerated, somehow contained within a compact vision.

The triumph of "Revelation" is its apparently natural unfolding of a series of quite extraordinary events, so that the impossibly smug, self-righteous Mrs. Turpin not only experiences a visual revelation but is prepared for it, demands it, and is equal to it in spite of her own bigotry. Another extraordinary aspect of the story is the protagonist's assumption—an almost automatic assumption—that the vicious words spoken to her by a deranged girl in a doctor's waiting room ("Go back to hell where you came from, you old wart hog") are in fact the words of Christ, intended for her alone. Not only is the spiritual world a literal, palpable fact but the physical world—of other people, of objects and events—becomes transparent, only a means by which the "higher" judgment is delivered. It is a world of meanings, naturalistic details crowded upon one another until they converge into a higher significance; an antinaturalistic technique, perhaps, but one which is firmly based in the observed world. O'Connor is always writing about Original Sin and the ways we may be delivered from it, and therefore she does not—cannot—believe in the random innocence of naturalism, which states that all men are innocent and are victims of inner or outer accidents. The naturalistic novel, which attempts to render the "real" world in terms of its external events, must hypothesize an interior randomness that is a primal innocence, antithetical to the Judaeo-Christian culture. O'Connor uses many of the sharply observed surfaces of the world, but her medieval sense of the *correspondentia* or the ancient "sympathy of all things" forces her to severely restrict her subject matter, compressing it to one or two physical settings and a few hours' duration. Since revelation can occur at any time and sums up, at the same time that it eradicates, all of a person's previous life, there is nothing claustrophobic about the doctor's waiting room, "which was very small," but which becomes a microcosm of an entire Godless society.

"Revelation" falls into two sections. The first takes place in the doctor's waiting room; the second takes place in a pig barn. Since so many who live now are diseased, it is significant that O'Connor chooses a doctor's waiting room for the first half of Mrs. Turpin's revelation, and it is significant that gospel hymns are being played over the radio, almost out of earshot, incorporated into the mechanical vacant listlessness of the situation: "When I looked up and He looked down . . . And wona these days I know I'll we-eara crown." Mrs. Turpin glances over the room, notices white-trashy people who are "worse than niggers any day," and begins a conversation with a well-dressed lady who is accompanying her daughter: the girl, on the verge of a breakdown, is reading a book called *Human Development,* and it is the book which will strike Mrs. Turpin in the forehead. Good Christian as she imagines herself, Mrs. Turpin cannot conceive of human beings except in terms of class, and is obsessed by a need to continually categorize others and speculate upon her position in regard to them. The effort is so exhausting that she often ends up dreaming "they were all crammed in together in a boxcar, being ridden off to be put in a gas oven." O'Connor's chilling indictment of Mrs. Turpin's kind of Christianity grows out of her conviction that the displacement of Christ will of necessity result in murder, but that the "murder" is a slow steady drifting rather than a conscious act of will.

The ugly girl, blue-faced with acne, explodes with rage at the inane bigotry expressed by Mrs. Turpin, and throws the textbook at her. She loses all control and attacks her; held down, subdued, her face "churning," she seems to Mrs. Turpin to know her "in some intense and personal way, beyond time and place and condition." And the girl's eyes lighten, as if a door that had been tightly closed was now open "to admit light and air." Mrs. Turpin steels herself, as if awaiting a revelation: and indeed the revelation comes. Mary Grace, used here by O'Connor as the instrument through which Christ speaks, bears some resemblance to other misfits in O'Connor's stories—not the rather stylish, shabby-glamorish men but the pathetic over-educated physically unattractive girls like Joy/Hulga of "Good Country People." That O'Connor identifies with these girls is obvious; it is *she,* through Mary Grace, who throws that textbook on human development at all of us, striking us in the forehead, hopefully to bring about a change in our lives.

Mrs. Turpin is shocked but strangely courageous. It is rare in O'Connor that an obtuse, unsympathetic character ascends to a higher level of self-awareness; indeed, she shows more courage than O'Connor's intellectual young men. She has been called a warthog from hell and her vision comes to her in the pig barn, where she stands above the hogs that appear to "pant with a secret life." It is these hogs, the secret panting mystery of life itself, that finally allow Mrs. Turpin to realize her vision. She seems to absorb from them some "abysmal life-giving knowledge" and, at sunset, she stares into the sky where she sees a vast swinging bridge extending upward from the earth through a field of living fire. Upon it a vast horde of souls were rumbling toward heaven. There were whole companies of white-trash, clean for the first time in their lives, and bands of black niggers in white robes, and battalions of freaks and lunatics shouting and clapping and leaping like frogs. And bringing up the end of the procession was a tribe of people whom she recognized at once as those who, like herself and Claude, had always had a little of everything. . . . They were marching behind the others with great dignity, accountable as they always had been for good order and common sense and respectable behavior. They alone were on key. Yet she could see by their shocked and altered faces that even their virtues were being burned away.

This is the most powerful of O'Connor's revelations, because it questions the very foundations of our assumptions of the ethical life. It is not simply our "virtues" that will be burned away but our rational faculties as well, and perhaps even the illusion of our separate, isolated egos. There is no way in which the ego can confront Mrs. Turpin's vision, except as she does — "her eyes small but fixed unblinkingly on what lay ahead." Like Teilhard, O'Connor is ready to acquiesce to the evolution of a form of higher consciousness that may be forcing itself into the world *at our expense;* as old Tarwater says, after he is struck and silenced by fire, "even the mercy of the Lord burns." Man cannot remain what he is; he cannot exist without being transformed. We are confronted, says Teilhard, with two directions and only two: one upward and the other downward.

Either nature is closed to our demands for futurity, in which case thought, the fruit of millions of years of effort, is stifled, still-born in a self-abortive and absurd universe. Or else an opening exists — that of the super-soul above our souls; but in that case the way out, if we are to agree to embark upon it, must open out freely onto limitless psychic spaces in a universe to which we can unhesitatingly entrust ourselves.

O'Connor's people are forced into the upward direction, sometimes against their wills, sometimes because their wills have been burned clean and empty. Rayber (*The Violent Bear It Away*), who has concentrated his love for mankind into a possessive, exaggerated love for an idiot child, is forced to contemplate a future without the "raging pain, the intolerable hurt that was his due"; he is at the core of O'Connor's vision, a human being who has suffered a transformation but who survives. The wisdom of the body speaks in us, even when it reveals to us a terrifying knowledge of Original Sin, a perversion of the blood itself.

O'Connor's revelations concern the mystic origin of religious experience, absolutely immune to any familiar labels of "good" and "evil." Her perverted saints are Kierkegaardian knights of the "absurd" for whom ordinary human behavior is impossible. Like young Tarwater, horrified at having said an obscenity, they are "too fierce to brook impurities of such a nature"; they are, like O'Connor herself, "intolerant of unspiritual evils. . . ." There is no patience in O'Connor for a systematic refined, rational acceptance of God; and of the gradual transformation of apocalyptic religious experience into dogma, she is strangely silent. Her world is that surreal primitive landscape in which the Unconscious is a determining quantity that the Conscious cannot defeat, because it cannot recognize. In fact, there is nothing to be recognized — there is only an experience to be suffered.

RALPH C. WOOD

From Fashionable Tolerance
to Unfashionable Redemption

Flannery O'Connor was preeminently a prophetic writer, a woman of apocalyptic vision. No matter how erroneously certain readers have sought to convert her art into theology, the fact remains that her work is religious to the core. One scants her fiction by reading it any other way — as, for example, the product of the Southern humorist tradition. The single religious concern woven through the tapestry of the entire O'Connor *oeuvre* is that the heedless secularity of the modern world deserves a withering judgment. It is fitting that "Judgement Day," Miss O'Connor's last completed story, should contain her central theme in its very title, thus bringing her career to an explicit culmination. But it is also surprising that this final story makes a break with the pattern of her previous fiction, thus opening up new possibilities which, alas, she did not live to realize.

I

Critics have often remarked the repetitive character of Flannery O'Connor's fiction. Over and again her stories are peopled with arrogant ingrates who suffer a harrowing encounter with their own presumption. When they are not purged with a grace which is consuming fire, they are left reeling with a startled sense of their own inadequacy. Neither readers nor characters can escape the searing judgment which stares from the tree line, the terrible wrath which blazes from the sky.

Only a bootless insolence could account for Miss O'Connor's stark vision as the result of psychological imbalance or sexual frustration. Neither does it suffice

From *The Flannery O'Connor Bulletin* 7 (Autumn 1978). © 1978 by *The Flannery O'Connor Bulletin*, Georgia College. Originally entitled "From Fashionable Tolerance to Unfashionable Redemption: A Reading of Flannery O'Connor's First and Last Stories."

to ascribe her prophetic outlook to a stunted imagination. It was not that O'Connor was unable to conceive a larger variety of characters and situations. She deliberately chose, I believe, to concentrate her art on what to her was the prime modern problem: the unprecedented apostasy whereby contemporary man has abandoned faith in anything transcending himself. Her fiction attempts, therefore, to bring harsh judgment upon a world determined to get along without an ultimate source of righteousness and redemption. Hence also the apocalyptic character of her work, where evil is depicted as becoming surpassingly sinister (and nonetheless, perhaps all the more comical), the hunger for grace increasingly ravenous, and the confrontation with mercy ever more violent.

It would seem, then, that Flannery O'Connor's fiction stands complete, despite the tragedy of her fatal disease. She wrote with a spiritual intensity which matched the awful certainty that she would die young, as if to make sure she utilized her prophetic imagination before her time elapsed. Yet only a year before her death, she declared to Sister Marietta Gable in a letter: "I've been writing for eighteen years and I've reached the point where I can't do again what I know I can do well, and the larger things that I need to do, I doubt my capacity for doing." She also asked her confessor to pray that she might be given new inspiration for her fiction, in virtual admission that she had exhausted its old possibilities.

I believe that Miss O'Connor's petition was at least partially granted. For her final story at once brings her fiction full circle and yet also makes the new departure she had prayed for. As if to signal the sea-change her fiction had undergone since its beginning in 1946, she seems consciously to have reworked the material of her first published story, "The Geranium." And what a revamping it is! For the final story not only corrects the errors of the earlier piece, it also points up the direction her work might have taken had she lived to complete it.

The setting for Flannery O'Connor's first and last stories is New York City, where two elderly Southern men have gone to live out their last years with their respective daughters. Each of the exiles is miserable in the confinement of apartment life, and the city itself is seen as a forbidding place, the very embodiment of a self-serving anonymity. The narrator of "Geranium," speaking from Old Dudley's standpoint, describes the frenzied facelessness of urban crowds: "People boiled out of trains and up steps and over into the streets. They rolled off the streets and down steps and into trains—black and white and yellow all mixed up like vegetables in soup." Nearly twenty years later the O'Connor narrator was to give old Tanner's similar judgment on his alien situation: "The window looked out on a brick wall and down into an alley full of New York air, the kind fit for cats and garbage."

In both stories the cold self-sufficiency of the city is made to seem all the
more damnable for having been adopted by Southerners accustomed to a more
humane way of life. And in electing such an abstract and unrooted existence,
the daughters have also married nondescript men who drive moving vans.
Alienated from their daughters, the lonely fathers wistfully recall the life they
enjoyed with their Negro friends in the South. This notwithstanding the fact
that, in the person of two Northern blacks, they both undergo dreadful confrontations with their own racial arrogance. But beyond these outward similarities,
the two stories bear little resemblance. "The Geranium" is a rather sentimental
and moralistic allegory, while "Judgement Day" is a penetrating piece of art.

The distance in the two stories can be seen in their respective narrators. The
authorial voice in "Geranium" seems to be a conventional moralist determined
to proclaim to both the reader and the chief character the gospel of human
brotherhood. Thus does Old Dudley painfully discover that Southern racial
zones are not observed in New York City, where Negroes can live next door to
whites. Unable to countenance such implicit equality with blacks, Dudley re-
buffs a well-mannered Negro's charitable offer to help him negotiate the long
apartment stairs. Finally the old man is reduced to literal apoplexy, and the
geranium in the window across the alley crashes to the ground as a heavy-handed
symbolic correlative to Dudley's shattered racial pride.

Such moral smugness and artistic crudity are utterly uncharacteristic of the
mature O'Connor. Hence her final story plumbs spiritual depths of which the
"Geranium" narrator seems wholly unaware. Dudley is a stock Southern character lifted out of Tennessee Williams or Carson McCullers, a doddering senti-
mentalist wishing for the good old days back South with his darky servants,
Rabie and Lutisha. Tanner in "Judgement Day" possesses a moral complexity
which makes his remembrance of his Negro friend Coleman anything but nos-
talgic. In the latter story, moreover, blacks and whites are found equally wanting
in the presence of a grace which makes mere racial tolerance seem, by comparison, something banal and unworthy.

In some respects "Judgement Day" fits the mold of vintage O'Connor fiction. Tanner's authentic (if flawed) faith and manners are set in favorable contrast to his daughter's heartless self-absorption and to the grim inhumanity of
the quintessential secular city. For all its reputed liberality, Northern society is
shown—at least as Tanner's daughter embodies it—to be deficient in family
solidarity, reverence for age and religion, particularity of character and place,
and the mutuality of social life: " 'Up here everybody minds their own business
and everybody gets along.' "

The experienced O'Connor reader naturally suspects that the daughter
awaits a frightening comeuppance, so that she will be made to see how vainly

she has cast off her rooted Southern values for the empty benefits of Northern urban existence. But no sooner have we begun to expect such an ordering of the story than we discover it taking an unexpected turn—one which sets it at odds both with a piece of juvenilia such as "Geranium," yet also with O'Connor's ripened work as well. To our sharp surprise, we find Southern racism receiving a far fiercer critique than New York secularism. More startling still, it is the faithful Tanner, not his unbelieving daughter, who faces the wrenching moment of grace. Most significant of all, grace is here depicted not only as searching sin out in anguishing revelation and purgation but also as seeking first to avert it in human mutuality. Yet the brotherhood here adumbrated has nothing to do with the facile tolerance advocated in "Geranium."

II

The spiritual depth and complexity of "Judgement Day" is evident in its mode of narration. As in *The Violent Bear It Away,* the opening scene is (unbeknownst to the reader) only a short remove from the conclusion. What appears, therefore, as a straightforward narrative is actually a series of convoluted flashbacks which account for Tanner's dilemma at the beginning and prepare for its resolution in the end. Thus already in the second paragraph Tanner is recalling what he did the previous day in preparation for his flight homeward. By the fourth paragraph O'Connor has plunged us into the first of five interwoven remembrances. Through them Tanner burrows ever more deeply into his own past, until finally he discerns the root of his misery, confronts the awfulness of his sin, and seizes his one hope for redemption and release.

The first of these recollections takes Tanner back into the immediate past when, two days earlier, he had learned how desperate his plight is. He had overheard his daughter and son-in-law declaring their intention to bury the old man in the city rather than take his body back to Georgia for its final rest. Their refusal to honor Tanner's desire for burial in his own native soil is more than filial ingratitude; it is a species of spiritual hubris. For the daughter has come to believe, in good secular fashion, that when we die we rot—it matters not where. When Tanner warns that such irreverence will land her in Hell, she hisses her disbelief in any such "hardshell Baptist hooey."

The heart of their conflict is thus not only familial but also religious, and the homecoming which old Tanner desires is less geographical than spiritual. But he will not experience it until he first confesses, if only inwardly, his own egregious pride. Tanner moves toward such penitence when, in a second remembrance ensconced within the first, he recalls his mistake in coming to live with his daughter in the first place. He had summoned her back to Corinth,

Georgia, to prevent his being humiliated by a black dentist who had bought the property on which he was squatting. There the daughter had found Tanner living in utter squalor with a Negro named Coleman. Although she had tried to shame her father for his disreputable life, he was at first able to resist her with his own splendidly reductive taunts: " 'You go on back up there. I wouldn't come with you for no million dollars or no sack of salt.' "

Then in a third descent into memory Tanner confesses, albeit still proudly, what prompted him to forsake his own true country for exile in New York. The sudden discovery that Negroes could buy land out from under whites was a shocking blow to Tanner's sense of racial superiority. The insolent black dentist represents, for Tanner, the ultimate reversal of values, the intrusion of Northern principles into Southern society, the placing of the bottom rail on the top. Rather than submit to such ignominy, he has come to reside with his daughter in New York. Could he make the decision over again, however, Tanner would gladly remain in Corinth, even if it meant becoming what he calls "a nigger's white nigger."

Far from humbling Tanner's racial presumption, this confession serves to reinforce it, as does his haughty declaration that he resisted the urge to kill the Negro doctor because he knew how to "handle niggers." There follows another remembrance (what amounts to a fourth flashback tucked into the third) wherein Tanner tells how he perfected his mastery of black men. It is, in my view, the most arresting episode in all of Flannery O'Connor's fiction, and it shows the workings of grace far more convincingly than reams of discourse on the subject. For what Tanner intends as a demonstration of his racial lordship turns into an unwitting account of that terrible moment of free choice when, against the entire spiritual grain of his being, he denied his fundamental companionship with another wretched creature who happened to be black.

It all began when a drunken Negro had wandered up to the isolated sawmill where Tanner was overseeing the work of six black laborers. Tanner did not fear the hulking Negro with muddy eyes, if only because he had always been able to dominate blacks by keeping before them a visible reminder of his sovereignty, a flashing blade:

> More than once he had stopped short and said in an off-hand voice to some half-reclining, head-averted Negro, "Nigger, this knife is in my hand now but if you don't quit wasting my time and money, it'll be in your gut shortly." And the Negro would begin to rise — slowly, but he would be in the act — before the sentence was completed.

When on the second day the loitering Negro had refused to leave, the white boss decided to put matters under control, lest his own tractable blacks be tempted to rebellion. But just as he had prepared to use the menace of the knife, Tanner unaccountably changed his mind. As if in fear that the giant Negro might turn on him in murderous wrath, Tanner had suddenly gone back to his whittling. Not with any deliberate design of his own but by the direction of an "intruding intelligence," Tanner found himself fashioning a crude pair of spectacles. With equal strangeness the Negro had momentarily put aside his own sense of alienation and begun watching Tanner's rough composition "as if he saw some invisible power working on the wood." Spurning the presence of these larger spiritual forces, Tanner had sought to taunt the hazy-eyed Negro into a conventional act of clownish submission: " 'You can't see so good, can you, boy? . . . Put these on,' he said, 'I hate to see anybody can't see good.' "

The addled Negro's instinctive reaction was to have crushed the fake glasses and Tanner with them. But in that very instant of rightful rage, there had been something else at work in him which offset the pleasure of thrusting the white man's knife into his innards. The innate sense of self-restraint which stayed the Negro's murderous hand prompted him to a further display of mutual regard which left Tanner even more perplexed. For in a mysterious act of willing self-humiliation, the black man put on the wood and haywire spectacles:

> He attached the bows carefully behind his ears and looked forth. He peered this way and that with exaggerated solemnity. And then he looked directly at Tanner and grinned, or grimaced, Tanner could not tell which, but he had an instant's sensation of seeing before him a negative image of himself, as if clownishness and captivity had been their common lot. The vision failed him before he could decipher it.

The Negro's minstrelsy may appear to be another instance of that "Tomming" and "signifying" by means of which Southern blacks have survived white oppression. Even if such buffoonery is a gesture of submission, I believe it is more a penitential than a racial act of obeisance. What the Negro acted out and what Tanner momentarily glimpsed was a mime of their essential condition: not their racial equality so much as their common imprisonment in the bonds of sin and mortality—as if they mirrored each other's mutual "clownishness and captivity." In acknowledging the absurdity of man's plight, the black man opened the way to real fellowship; in denying their comic desperation, Tanner cut himself off from both an immediate and an ultimate communion. The one saw truly despite his liquored eyes and lensless glasses, while the other blinded himself to ultimate truth.

I find this scene deeply convincing because it dramatizes the operation of grace in an ordinary situation, the mysterious within the commonplace, the supernatural amidst the mundane. The revelation may come here as an invisible intrusion upon the two men from without, but it also arises from the depths of their hearts. There is no need for theological assertion because the scene enacts the movements of a grace which, implicitly at least, seeks to offer itself to men at every moment of their lives and which, would they not spurn it, might bind them together in true companionship.

The larger significance of this life-turning encounter was not wholly lost on Tanner. For while he recalls the incident as an instance of his ability to "handle niggers," it establishes exactly the opposite. The Negro's mimicry broke the tension between them and led to a chaffing exchange of witticisms which proved him not to be another anonymous "nigger" but a human being named Coleman. Even if the deeper meaning of Coleman's confession of their mutual misery remained opaque to Tanner, they became life companions from that moment forward. For the sake of his own threatened pride, Tanner still maintains that Coleman was a lackey who could not resist the white man's domination. But we know how sorely Tanner now misses Coleman, how wistfully he dreams of him. Thus while Coleman may have indeed played the role of the monkey on Tanner's back, one suspects he did so less in abject servility than in sardonic admission of their common captivity.

III

This series of interwoven flashbacks culminates in Tanner's fifth and final meditation, wherein he recalls his recent clash with the black man living in the adjacent apartment. The previous recollections prepare for this last one, both fictionally and spiritually. Not only is Tanner's mind gradually moving toward the present and readying itself for the fearful future which awaits him, it also links his Northern and Southern encounters with Negroes as mutually revelatory. Having set out originally to justify his mistaken decision to live with his daughter, Tanner comes dimly to recognize how the wrath which falls on him in New York is a kind of punishment for the mercy which he rejected in Georgia years ago. It was, as it were, the original sin which has corrupted the whole of his life.

As if in penance for having abandoned his Negro companion in Georgia, Tanner had tried to befriend the Negro next door, naïvely thinking him to be a fellow exile wishing to be back in the South. Tanner had greeted him with the familiar term of endearment which Southerners often (and without condescension) used to address black men: "Preacher." Stung both by Tanner's easy familiarity and by the spiritual assumptions implicit in it, this secularized Nothern Negro spat back a mouthful of invective which reveals how deeply Tanner's greeting had struck home:

When he was close enough he lunged and grasped Tanner by both shoulders. "I don't take no crap," he whispered, "off no wool-hat red-neck son-of-a-bitch peckerwood old bastard like you." He caught his breath. And then his voice came out in the sound of an exasperation so profound that it rocked on the verge of a laugh. It was high and piercing and weak. "And I'm not no preacher! I'm not even no Christian. I don't believe that crap. There ain't no Jesus and there ain't no God."

It is a mark of Tanner's integrity that he did not forego honesty for friendliness by seeking to soothe the black man's anger. The Negro had repudiated the deepest truth of all, and Tanner was determined to let him know the folly of such a denial: "The old man felt his heart inside him hard and tough as an oak knot. 'And you ain't black,' he said. 'And I ain't white!'" Such truthfulness served further to enrage the black man, who struck Tanner with such violence as to induce in him a stroke.

Given Tanner's racist history, one would expect such a scourging to issue in an irremediable hatred of blacks and perhaps an enduring bitterness toward life itself. Remarkably, however, there is no rancor in Tanner's remembrance of this horrific episode. He reports the incident almost neutrally, and not with the indignation he had earlier felt toward the black dentist, even though he has more cause for vengeance now than then. By linking the beating to his earlier encounters with black men, moreover, Tanner seems implicitly to acknowledge it as a kind of purgation, a terrible penance for failing to decipher the grace Coleman proffered him in pantomine—indeed, for the accumulated arrogance of his life.

In the first speechless days following the stroke-inducing attack, Tanner had made his ultimate peace and was reconciled to the death he knew was soon to come. He had even dreamed of going home alive in a pine coffin and of jumping out to startle his friends at the Corinth train depot with a joke: "'Judgement Day! Judgement Day! . . . Don't you two fools know it's Judgement Day?'" But O'Connor will not let Tanner die amidst such roguish dreams. As the story finally returns to the opening scene, he faces a day of judgment which is not feigned but real. For he has overheard his daughter and son-in-law planning to bury him in New York rather than heeding his desire to rest in his own soil. It is this shocking discovery, this final betrayal—not the Negro's brutal assault—which moves Tanner to set out desperately for Georgia on his own, "as confident as if the woods lay at the bottom of the stairs."

Externally, Tanner's hope is the emptiest illusion. He has no chance of making it back to Georgia alone, and the frustration of his last earthly desire would seem to deny any ultimate hope as well. Flannery O'Connor's final task, therefore, is to show how Tanner's faith is fictionally as well as religiously valid, despite everything that counts against it and without authorial commentary merely asserting it to be such. In my view she accomplishes this task admirably by preparing for Tanner's redemptive death through the interconnected flashbacks in which he reluctantly owns up to his sin and yet does willing penance for it. Surely this hard-won faith is the source of Tanner's extraordinary confidence as he stumbles out of his daughter's apartment with his heart thumping like "a great heavy bell whose clapper swung from side to side but made no noise." Despite the terrible knowledge that he will not get to the New York train station, much less to Corinth, Georgia, Tanner walks through the valley of the shadow of death fearing no evil, not even an anonymous grave in a loathsome place. He is bound for a City (to cite the Psalter Tanner apparently knows by heart) not made with hands but eternal in the heavens.

When Tanner collapses into what will be his ending, he dreams not of a *dies irae* but of the casket trick and its jaunty punch line. Nor is he disturbed by the jeers of the black man next door, who taunts dying Tanner with the doubt that there is no ultimate reckoning, only the animal extinction he is now facing. Freed of all fear and ready to die even at the hands of this heartless Negro, Tanner again addresses him as "Preacher," asks for his help, and makes his final affirmation of faith: " 'I'm on my way home.' "

Evidently scandalized by the pathos of the old man's dying condition and surely offended by his truculent faith, the black actor apparently subjected Tanner to a last humiliation. For when Tanner's daughter returns from the grocery, she finds her father dead, his head and arms stuffed through the banister, his legs dangling "over the stairwell like a man in stocks." O'Connor chooses wisely not to narrate this final brutality, but to report it indirectly from the daughter's point of view. Rather than making the reader wince at the infliction of such torment, the already finished violence may serve as a quiet reminder of another Humiliation, where also the significance lay not so much in the pain suffered as in the atonement wrought.

There is, however, no extraneous theologizing from Miss O'Connor, no attempt to make Tanner into a Christ figure who somehow reenacts the Passion in modern secular form. Instead, the story's title echoes throughout the latter part of the narrative to suggest how Tanner's initial hope is realized in the end. His final degradation notwithstanding, he has made his way home. The entire action of the story bears this affirmation out: Tanner has confessed his sin (albeit unwittingly in a series of remembrances meant to justify his racial pride), received his judgment, done his penance, and thus gone to his eternal destiny well prepared.

It is such a triumphant completion, despite the macabre death, that O'Connor ends the story with an extraordinarily light touch. No sooner has the daughter buried her father in New York than she is stricken by her act of bad faith. In her own small show of penitence, she has his body disinterred and sent back to Georgia for burial. "Now," we are told, "she rests well at night and her good looks have mostly returned." This sardonic conclusion serves as a zany contrast to Tanner's own description of her "flat dumb face." More importantly, it prevents any tragic reading of the story as the account of a pathetic creature meeting his sad end among aliens in an alien place. There is, on the contrary, hardly a more jubilant story in Flannery O'Connor's work.

The distance between "The Geranium" and "Judgement Day" is not a matter, spiritually and artistically, of decades but of light years. The youthful O'Connor had rightly seen, in her first story, that men desperately need to be reconciled to one another, but without discerning the means for true fellow-feeling. So in her last story she recast her early material into a treatment of human reconciliation which is profound and convincing to the same degree that her first story seems callow and naïve. This latter vision of human communion is rooted in precisely the need which had earlier been ignored: not for men to tolerate each other in equality but to be redeemed in a common humility and forgiveness.

Tanner wins through to such a redemption of his own sinful past and to an acceptance of a grisly death only after a slow and painful self-recognition. Perhaps it is not inappropriate to regard Tanner's spiritual journey as being similar to Flannery O'Connor's own, and to view this story as her final testament in the face of her ultimate extremity. There is no question but that "Judgement Day" is a splendid capstone on her whole career, bringing it back full circle to the point where it began. For while this story sounds her old theme of judgment and wrath, it also breaks new fictional ground which, sadly, she never lived to till. In the end it was given Flannery O'Connor to narrate convincingly what she had known all along but never fictionally embodied: that the world is not so much assaulted as redeemed by grace, and that the final as well as the first word it speaks to man is not No but Yes.

CAROL SHLOSS

Epiphany

And this, as I could not prevail on any of my actors to speak, I was obliged to declare myself.

HENRY FIELDING, *Tom Jones*

Flannery O'Connor never wrote a first-person narrative, nor did she ever completely surrender her third-person prose to the limitations of a subjective point of view. She undertook the offices of writer with all the freedoms of traditional storytelling, assuming the omniscient manipulation of fictional destinies with an unquestioning ease. One wonders if she could have written otherwise, for a subjective perspective in fiction writing narrows the authority of the given account; it implies that there can be another point of view, a different set of meanings to assigned events. In turn, this relativity suggests that one can live in doubt, that one can live, as Lionel Trilling has said, "by means of a question" instead of by an unassailable religious persuasion.

This was exactly what O'Connor did not want to do — to concede that there could be more than one viable interpretation of reality. In her opinion, conflicts between ways of being constituted a challenge to Christian truth that could not be brooked, and with this certainty of outlook, she reserved final narrative authority for herself. For the hard of hearing she would "shout," for the blind she would "draw large and startling figures." Yet with all this allusion to rhetoric, to bold and unambiguous fictional strategies, O'Connor was curiously reluctant to exploit the potential of the omniscient voice. Rarely in all these tales of bizarre

From *Flannery O'Connor's Dark Comedies: The Limits of Inference.* © 1980 by Louisiana State University Press.

65

and violent experience does she reflect on the meaning of the grotesquery or give explicit value to fictional events. She infrequently enunciates in her fictional world what she had no trouble conveying in personal life — that Christian orthodoxy was the consistent measure of experience. This is usually left for the reader to infer, to come upon through the indirections of allusion, incongruities, and distorted hyperbole.

As must be clear by now, I have the image of O'Connor creating her audience from her own fears and isolation, creating a composite image from antagonistic reviews that arrived in the mail, conjuring a reader who was not only ignorant but, like so many of the characters of her own imagination, resistant to her theological point of view. Any author as removed from live, intelligent, and informed readership as O'Connor was must evolve a complicated kind of "double-think" to deal with this distance. As Martha Stephens has noticed, "Flannery O'Connor seems to have sought, all her writing life, a means of approach to an audience whose religious sense she believed to be stunted and deformed." She thought as a Christian and wrote as a Christian while constantly second-guessing her "monstrous reader," anticipating the workings of a mind that did not know by experience or explicit heritage the forms and assumptions of Christianity. But I would like to suggest that to "shout" in fiction about any belief, Christian or otherwise, is done effectively, not by leaving norms or opinions implicit in the text, reachable if at all through inference, but by interpreting events explicitly, through the privileges of the omnisciently narrated tale, or by making man's encounter with religion the explicit topic of exposition. There is a limit to what one can infer from a text, just as there is a limit to what can be accepted in writing. It was in the precarious territory where one neither offended nor obscured by excessive indirection that I think O'Connor tried to live artistically.

Perhaps O'Connor's reluctance to take full advantage of the possibilities of omniscient narration was the result of her own "double-thinking," her anxiety that hostile readers or astute critics would take offense at open preachments; perhaps it arose in response to her own belief that dramatization is a more effective narrative procedure than straight address to the reader. She was unlike Graham Greene, who had the same concern to manipulate judgment but did not hesitate to comment directly when he sensed, in *Brighton Rock,* for example, that readers might apply the conventional standards of right and wrong rather than the required standards of good and evil. He distinguished carefully between the pitiable but blessed "hole" where Rose lived, knowing "murder, copulation, extreme poverty, fidelity and the love and fear of God," and the glaring "open world outside" where people like Ida made a false claim to experience. Whatever the source of her reticence, O'Connor tried most often simply to enact the experience of revelation in her fiction, hoping that the implications of dramatized events would be self-evident. However, the limitations on a reader's understanding of these revelations is imposed directly by her handling of them. For time and again—in "Greenleaf," "Good Country People," "A Circle in the Fire," "Parker's Back," "A View of the Woods"—the protagonist is taken to the point of profound insight and then is killed or simply abandoned by an author who apparently fears that denouement will lessen the impact of undeniably dramatic events. The reader is left, then, with a burden, with a brooding sense of weight, of ominous importance whose source is ultimately ambiguous, unlocatable in clearly defined experience. For as talented as O'Connor is at rendering the violent and profound moment, she is nonetheless unable or unwilling to dramatize states of consciousness, to take her readers inside the mind of the perceiving character and show them what exactly has been experienced. Virginia Woolf thought this was unimportant. Katharine in the novel *Night and Day* remarks that it is "the process of discovering" that matters, "not the discovery itself." But this cannot be said of O'Connor, for whom, presumably, the content of the revelation was everything. As the following discussion will show, the revelation of epiphany that occurs outside a specifically theological fictional context is left open to a variety of interpretations ("Revelation"), and the revelation that occurs within the parameters of religious quest can still be unsatisfactory ("Parker's Back"). It is only when the author takes it upon herself to expose the thoughts and perceptions of characters in the presence of grace that an unequivocal meaning is accessible to the reader. Although O'Connor may have feared this authorial direction, her infrequent assumption of the role of commentator results in some of the finest passages in her work. For we have at these rare moments a sense of character rendered with sympathy and gladness; human beings are held up in their best hours to be admired instead of judged.

Since the art of any fiction is essentially an art of revelation, some definitions are called for. To begin with, there is a distinction between the gradual disclosure that all stories effect and a revelation to a character that is specific in time and intense in effect. As Morris Beja observes in his book *Epiphany in the Modern Novel,* until the last centuries, *epiphany* identified the moments in which an external force revealed some truth to human beings. But at present the word has come to have a quite different application, especially since it was appropriated by Joyce, who adapted the religious pattern and terminology to secular experience. In *Stephen Hero,* Joyce's autobiographical novel, the author defines his term. Although the passage is familiar and often quoted, it is useful to cite it in this context, if only to contrast it with O'Connor's own understanding of the word. Stephen identifies an epiphany as "a sudden spiritual manifestation, whether in the vulgarity of speech or of gesture or in a memorable phrase of the mind itself. He believed that it was for the man of letters to record these epiphanies, with extreme care, seeing that they themselves are the most delicate and evanescent of moments." Later in the novel Stephen clarifies the idea when he expresses the belief that this manifestation may be produced by "an ordinary concrete object, a work of art, a snatch of talk overheard on the street, a gesture."

Far from being oracular—the voice of a hidden god intruding on the human world—the source of Joyce's epiphany is the human commonplace. Although the stuff of ordinary life occasions sudden illumination, no one may count on such insights. For objects are not "active," impinging forcibly on consciousness. In fact, it is normal to take them for granted. But a sensitive perceiver can effect a transformation, finding suddenly and intuitively the unnoticed value, the hidden meaning. In Joyce's terminology, the artist, the astute perceiver, is a priest who "converts the daily bread of experience into the radiant body of everlasting life." Notice the inversion of the religious concept. Epiphany is no longer a passive human experience—the revelation of a god who is active—as, for example, Paul's revelation and conversion on the Damascus road was passive. Rather, Joyce emphasizes the role of man's mind and imagination. What is revealed is not divinity in the classic sense of an independent deity but a timeless brilliance previously unperceived; or it is the self that is seen with harsh honesty, as when the boy in "Araby" realizes that his illusions about the fair are not the only ones he has harbored: "Gazing up into the darkness, I saw myself as a creature driven and derided by vanity; and my eyes burned with anguish and anger." In effect, Joyce celebrates the marriage of the sacred and the profane, for the things that are "holy" are precisely those conditions of life that ordinarily seem familiar and squalid. These manifestations are sacred not in a theological sense (deriving from divine grace) but figuratively. Hence the word *spiritual* is used by Joyce only to evoke a sense of submerged meaning, the quality of inner life that is brought to light.

This same celebration of the commonplace is an implicit motive in Virginia Woolf's novel *To the Lighthouse,* and it is also the topic of reflection for at least one of the characters, the painter Lily Briscoe, who observes, "One wishes to feel simply that's a chair, that's a table and yet at the same time, it's a miracle, it's an ecstasy." And at another time, Lily reflects: "The great revelation had never come. The great revelation perhaps never did come. Instead, there were little daily miracles, illuminations, matches struck unexpectedly in the dark."

To both of these authors, the epiphany was evanescent, delicate. The common things of life were the only components of human experience. Because no larger framework of established meaning existed to lend them weight, the discovery of meaning in the things themselves was the work of creative intelligence. They would have both sympathized with Proust's Marcel, who realized, tasting the madeleine dipped in tea, "It is plain that the object of my quest, the truth, lies not in the cup but in myself."

But O'Connor did not use Joyce or Woolf as her models. For her, Lily Briscoe's "great revelation" did come; in fact, it was the central human experience. All the matches struck in the dark were, by contrast, so many subjective delusions. We can deduce from O'Connor's work her concurrence with the notion that truth is concealed from us except in extraordinary circumstances, but her portrayal of the nature of that truth or the manner of its disclosure reveals a sensibility radically removed from either Joyce's or Woolf's. She seemed to feel more of an affinity with the ancient concept of epiphany, and hence she tended to emphasize a divine movement-human response pattern, whereby people are no longer agents of epiphany through the movements of their minds but the recipients of some great and even unsought knowledge.

In the fiction these beliefs are recognizable in the narrative patterns of stories. No matter how much an O'Connor protagonist may grumble and bustle about, attending to her fate, the decisive life experience is thrust upon her. A bull rams her; a Negress smashes her; she is captured and shot by a criminal. In all of these tales, the emphasis in the narrative is on human response, on the posture assumed before external force. From this concentration ensues a cumulative sense of human impotence, a suggestion of the inefficacy of self-direction. There is reason to believe that O'Connor understood this passivity to be a virtue. In the introduction to the 1962 edition of *Wise Blood,* she asked rhetorically: "Does one's integrity ever lie in what he is not able to do? I think that it does." And in her letters, she wrote about passive diminishment, about accepting unalterable limitations. But to the reader, this is a disquieting attitude with ambiguous implications.

This sense of life as response rather than action is further reinforced by a rhetorical habit perhaps used unconsciously—a tendency not only to use the passive voice but to describe characters as victims of their own perceptions, as persons accosted by sight and sound rather than simple perceivers. In "Greenleaf," Mrs. May is the target of her own sight; the sun becomes "narrow and pale until it looked like a bullet. Then suddenly it burst through the treeline and raced down the hill toward her." Likewise in "The River," Bevel, drowning in the river, is pursued by the same kind of active vision. "Mr. Paradise's head appeared from time to time on the surface of the water. Finally, far downstream, the old man rose like some ancient water monster and stood empty-handed." If the intention in writing is to create the sense of an unseen, undramatizable divine grace, one way to suggest its presence is certainly through human response to it. Hence the use of passive voice and the intrusion of sight can be regarded as plausible attempts to define by reaction. But again, this is a negative strategy, an acknowledgment that we do not have words for all that is thought to exist. The author "cannot describe what he sees; he can only point to the place where it appears to be." In this circumstance, the audience's expectation of supernatural meaning must be "so strong that a failure within language indicates the reality of something beyond language." The absence of this expectation (and it would be absent in an agnostic readership) leaves room to ascribe various motivations to this general human passivity, especially since O'Connor provides examples of sight violating the onlooker in undoubtedly secular situations, as when Hazel Motes is driving through the country in *Wise Blood*. "The sky leaked over all of it and then began to leak into the car. The head of a string of pigs appeared snout-up over the windowshield and he had to screech to a stop and watch the rear of the last pig disappear shaking into the ditch on the other side." This tendency to use the same technique to represent both potentially religious experience and decidedly nonreligious circumstances parallels O'Connor's use of the grotesque to describe both the "sacred" and the "damned." The indiscriminate use of distorted rendering can result in ambiguous control of a reader's sympathy. In a recent critique, Miles Orvel commented, "It was well that O'Connor had this tradition for it would help her to solve what would be her chief literary problem — how to embody . . . the godly ungrand [quester], the man whose distortion signifies that God, through his grace, is alive in him." But it is difficult to accept this reasoning when ungrand, ungodly men are represented in the same unwieldy terms. Similarly, the perpetually responsive posture of many of these O'Connor characters, religiously obsessed and otherwise, does not lead inevitably to the supposition that their reactions are always to grace but often simply to the conclusion that they are victimized.

The following sections will illustrate these problems as they occur in stories explicitly about the religious experience, or in fictional occasions wherein epiphany (in the old non-Joycean sense of the truth actively revealing itself) is an active principle of storytelling.

II

It is a tribute to O'Connor's "reasonable use of the unreasonable" that, in "Revelation," she could make a bite on a fat woman's neck by a Wellesley student with acne the occasion for self-confrontation. After the attack and before she is drugged, the ugly girl whispers to Mrs. Turpin, "Go back to hell where you come from, you old wart hog!" This farfetched accusation shapes the remaining story, as Mrs. Turpin strives to understand in what sense she can possibly be a pig. "How am I a hog and me both? How am I saved and from hell too?" And, as she ponders these questions, gazing down into the pig parlor on her farm, "as if through the very heart of mystery," the answer comes to her. Her vision is as extraordinary as the events that have preceded it, and it is posed in terms that are equally stark and funny.

She saw the streak as a vast swinging bridge extending upward from the earth through a field of living fire. Upon it a vast horde of souls were rumbling toward heaven. There were whole companies of white-trash clean for the first time in their lives, the bands of black niggers in white robes, and battalions of freaks and lunatics shouting and clapping and leaping like frogs. And bringing up the end of the procession was a tribe of people whom she recognized at once as those who, like herself and Claud, had always had a little of every-thing and the God-given wit to use it right. She leaned forward to observe them closer. They were marching behind the others with great dignity, accountable as they had always been for good order and common sense and respectable behavior. They alone were on key. Yet she could see by their shocked and altered faces that even their virtues were being burned away. She lowered her hands.

As infrequently happens in O'Connor stories, the content of Mrs. Turpin's revelation is fully externalized; it is made as available to the reader as to the fic-tional recipient. Unlike Mrs. May's encounter in "Greenleaf," or Mrs. Cope's ex-perience at the end of "A Circle in the Fire," we do not have to construe the probable nature of the suffering insight. It is a decided step toward rendering of subjective consciousness; nonetheless, the nature of the vision, even when it is unmistakably exposed, has its own set of accompanying ambiguities. To under-stand why, consider the context of this disturbing revelation.

It is the result of a shock to a respectable woman's self-image. O'Connor begins the story in a doctor's office, and the patients waiting for attention constitute a microcosm of southern society. The chance gathering, the situation of persons unknown to each other assembled in a room, could provide a forum for discussing the workings of fate (in the way that Thornton Wilder asks why five particular people were together on the bridge of San Luis Rey when it broke), but O'Con-nor arranges this cast to reflect the workings of Mrs. Turpin's mind. In this room are all the possibilities of birth and position in the rural South: a well-dressed, "pleasant" lady; a thin, worn woman in a cheap cotton dress; another woman in a "gritty-looking" yellow sweatshirt and slacks; a dirty sniveling child; a fat, ugly teenager; and eventually a black messenger boy. Her presence in this company occasions one of Mrs. Turpin's frequent reflections on the good fortune of her own position in life, and this extends into the question of who she would have chosen to be if she couldn't have been herself. "If Jesus had said to her before he made her, 'There's only two places available to you. You can either be a nigger or white-trash,' what would she have said?" In the imaginative interior mono-logue that follows, Mrs. Turpin reveals both the source of her self-satisfaction and her criterion of evaluation: she considers herself a good woman, a hard worker, clean and charitable; she would rather be a black woman with these qualities than "white-trash." When confronted with the imaginative alternative of being born ugly, she is horrified. Although Mrs. Turpin does not articulate these thoughts, O'Connor counterpoints the woman's private musings with what is said, to tell the reader what is actually behind the public facade. For example, when Mrs. Turpin says she and Claud have a pig parlor and a hose to wash down the pigs, she thinks to herself that her animals are cleaner than the snot-nosed child. When a poorly dressed woman says she "wouldn't scoot down no hog with no hose," Mrs. Turpin thinks, "You wouldn't have no hog to scoot down." This discrepancy between private opinion and public comment acts as an effective signal of hypocrisy and shows, without any explicit authorial comment, the distance between Mrs. Turpin's complacency and her faults. Where the woman sees herself as charitable, she is shown to be proud; where she considers herself thoughtful, she is condescending; her solicitousness hides contempt. In terms of both race and class, Mrs. Turpin's self-satisfaction is gained at the expense of others. Although she does not expose herself directly, she insinuates enough for the Wellesley student to surmise the truth, to assault her physically, and to accuse her of being a wart hog.

It is at this juncture that Mrs. Turpin tries to come to terms with the accusation. " 'I am not,' she said tearfully, 'a wart hog. From hell.' " That the denial has no force shows the protagonist to be moving toward a recognition of the distortion that the reader already has seen. The final vision of souls "rumbling toward heaven" is posed in exactly the terms in which Mrs. Turpin has always seen life, as a matter of social hierarchy. But she envisions herself to be last in line; this time in procession behind the white-trash, Negroes, and lunatics, and it is this image that completes the message of ill-founded self-esteem.

If one wishes to identify grace as that which destroys illusions, then it can be said that Mrs. Turpin has experienced grace. But to say this is very different from making a statement about religion, for the epiphanies that occur in Joyce's fiction can be described in the same way. What is different is the tone and theatricality of O'Connor's moment of insight. In Joyce's work, a young boy looks up at the dim ceiling of a closing fair and says quietly, "I saw myself as a creature driven and derided by vanity." In O'Connor's work, this same realization of vanity is heralded by ponderous machinery. "She raised her hand from the side of the pen in a gesture hieratic and profound. A visionary light settled in her eyes. She saw." The vision that is subsequently revealed is not couched in personal terms; Mrs. Turpin does not see herself as the boy in "Araby" did. She only recognized "those who like herself . . . had always had a little of everything." It should be noticed that the revelation is a dramatization of a hypothetical event—a parade to heaven; it is not the actual statement of understanding. Consequently, the abstract meaning of this imaginative parade, both to Mrs. Turpin and to the reader, is still left to be construed. That the march is to heaven and the language theological is undeniable. But the vision occurs in the idiom that has characterized this woman's previous musings; the terms of formulation are consistent with the character of the churchgoing middle class, and in this respect the whole imaginary scene can be considered a metaphor, the concrete terms of an abstraction that remains unstated in the text. The meaning of the vision, then, is not forced into the mold of theology; for the language and images of theology are used as a means to an end that must answer the problems posed in the preceding events of the story. What Mrs. Turpin must see as she turns from the pigsty is her own participation in lowlife, her own complicity, along with blacks and poor whites, in human suffering and limitation. This is what had remained beyond her self-image in the doctor's waiting room; this is the knowledge that presumably can diminish her complacency. For the reader, the fact that the "message" has been given to Ruby Turpin, "a respectable, hard-working, churchgoing woman," has its own implications. For it suggests that the most self-respecting people can also be the most dangerous.

III

In the story "Revelation," the secular context of the protagonist's vision served as a guide to the interpretation of that vision. Even if O'Connor had intended that the vision be considered to come from God and to be concerned with Mrs. Turpin's salvation, the evidence is ambiguous. Because the theological norms of behavior are often the norms of society, Mrs. Turpin's faults can be recognized as faults simply by virtue of her deviance from the publicly admired traits of honesty and humility. However, there are occasions when the problems faced in the fictional situation are more specifically religious; one such narrative is "Parker's Back." O'Connor wrote this, her last story, on her deathbed in the Piedmont Hospital, and there is a telling anecdote about the circumstances of its composition. Caroline Gordon went to visit Flannery several weeks before she died and found her weak but cheerfully able to report, as she pulled a pad and pencil from under her pillow, that the doctor wouldn't let her work, but it was all right for her to write a little fiction. The irony of the situation is apparent, as is O'Connor's remarkable and admirable obsession with writing. But these extreme circumstances reveal not only a writer's dedication but her desperation; for the story is contrived, its message offered at the expense of credibility.

The discovery of inconsistency or incompleteness on the literal level of a narrative can lead to a search for meaning on a secondary, nonliteral level of exposition. In "Parker's Back," the realistic inconsistencies of the text are so apparent that it is impossible to follow a "natural symbolism" of events, to construe satisfactorily the inherent meanings of actions. Reference to a value system external to the text is the only way to find any coherence in the narrative, and since the subject of the story is the symbolic representation of God, those meanings are unambiguously religious.

"Parker's Back" is a story of a search for the roots of personal dissatisfaction. There are two epiphanies in the narrative (in Joyce's sense of moments of heightened consciousness), and along with these quiet realizations, there is a cataclysmic event that hurls the protagonist irrevocably into an altered awareness. The trauma in O. E. Parker's life is a farming accident: he absentmindedly drives a tractor into a huge tree, is hurled from the machine screaming "God above!" and watches as tractor, tree, and his own shoes burn. O'Connor tells us that "he could feel the hot breath of the burning tree on his face" as if the tree were animated with an intimate message, and that O. E. immediately careens away from the scene and heads toward the city in his truck. "Parker did not allow himself to think on the way to the city. He only knew that there had been a great change in his life, a leap into a worse unknown, and that there was nothing he could do about it." The narration of this crisis is typical of O'Connor's handling of revelation. The character is passive, the experience is both unanticipated and unwanted. Something unspecified but disturbing has happened to his mind. But however much O.E. Parker may sense his own altered circumstances, his reaction is the programmed, mechanical solution that he has had for all of his internal anguish: he will get another tattoo.

The pattern of the narrative is, then, a pattern of obsession briefly but decisively interrupted. All of O. E.'s previous anxieties have been solved, at least temporarily, by getting a new tattoo. The colored images are each pleasing to O. E., and collectively they contribute to his goal of becoming like a tattoo artist he had seen as a boy. In flashback the reader is told that O. E. had seen the performer "flexing his muscles so that the arabesque of men and beasts and flowers on his skin appeared to have a subtle emotion, lifted up." Of this first epiphany O'Connor tells us not only that he was moved but why. "Until he saw the man at the fair, it did not enter his head that there was anything out of the ordinary about the fact that he existed . . . [it was] as if a blind boy had been turned so gently in a different direction that he did not know his destination had been changed." In this instance, O'Connor makes full use of the omniscient voice, exposing both the subjective impression of the character and more than the character could possibly have divined (that the experience was in some way definitive). But the implications of this brief allusion to the change in Parker's life are obscure. For the "different direction" appears to be nothing more than a home cure; O. E. has acquired a remedy for his recurring dissatisfactions.

Just as the urge to engrave his body is irrational, so is Parker's marriage to a sallow religious fundamentalist. This woman, Sarah Ruth, questions Parker's tattooing impulse. "At the judgement seat of God, Jesus is going to say to you, 'What you been doing all your life besides have pictures drawn all over you?'" She prefers him covered up or in the dark. It is a strange, strained union, initiated irrationally and continued irrationally; Parker especially is perplexed by his motivation for staying with such a woman.

Thus an obsession with tattoos and a preoccupation with pleasing a sour wife precede the trauma of Parker's accident, and these things shape his response to it. He will tattoo the image of Christ on his back, resolving his own anxiety about the accident in the accustomed manner and hoping also to please Sarah Ruth. After all, he reasons, "She can't say she don't like the looks of God." To this point, this character's motivation is farfetched, improbable, but consistent. It is precisely at this point that O'Connor effects a radical change in his perception. The tattoo assumes an added significance to Parker, as if the psychic change that he had sought to effect with other pictures has finally been achieved. It is clear that the tattoo is not a picture of Christ but an image with a keenly felt moral imperative. "Parker sat for a long time . . . examining his soul. He saw it as a spider web of facts and lies that was not at all important to him but which appeared to be necessary in spite of his opinion. The eyes that were forever on his back were eyes to be obeyed. He was as certain of it as he had ever been of anything." This insight into the vanity of his previous life, the irrational identification of a tattoo with a command, is then shown to be identical to other unaccountable impulses. "Throughout his life, grumbling and sometimes cursing, often afraid, once in rapture, Parker had obeyed whatever instinct of this kind had come to him — in rapture when his spirit had lifted at the sight of the tattooed man at the fair, afraid when he had joined the navy, grumbling when he had married Sarah Ruth." The second epiphany contains, then, the key to all of Parker's previous conduct; it reveals, as it were, a theme of the life, locating his feeling about the Christ tattoo in the larger context of his vulnerability toward the forces of irrationality. In the remaining narrative, Parker comes to terms with the implications of his new emotional allegiance, first by denying it in the face of his buddies' ridicule, then by identifying himself to his wife with his biblical name, Obadiah. The scene where Parker tries to gain entrance to his locked home, the scene where he acknowledges the new self by use of the new name, is rendered with the same hyperbolic dramatic machinery that had accompanied Mrs. Turpin's revelation. "The sky had lightened slightly and there were two or three streaks of yellow floating above the horizon. Then as he stood there, a tree of light burst over the skyline. Parker fell back against the door as if he had been pinned there by a lance." The tree of light completes the insight begun by the burning tree in the farm accident; Parker recognizes himself as an Obadiah and, with this, receives the assurance that his choice is correct. At this moment, his "spider web soul turned into a perfect arabesque of colors, a garden of trees and birds and beasts." The language echoes that used previously to describe the tattoo artist's exterior. Here, however, the condition described is an internal one; the language suggests metaphorically a lively harmony and, with it, a sense of peace, the implied end to a disgruntled quest. What had been sought as a condition of the body is received as a condition of the soul. The inversion is complete.

The story, however, is not completed with this reversal. Instead, O'Connor finishes the action in terms of Parker and Sarah Ruth's marital relationship. The wife, good fundamentalist that she has always been, rejects the "face of God" on Parker's back. To her, as to everyone of that religious persuasion, any image of God is a metaphor to be used, if at all, to assist the imagination. For her it contains no moral imperative. She beats her husband, raising welts on his back and consequently on this image. Parker ends this episode of his life under one of the trees that has been so important to him, in tears.

If we can accept the harshness of Sarah Ruth's character, the extremity of Parker's obsessions, and O'Connor's idea of what marriage is like, the story has some vague psychological coherence. Parker cries because a gesture intended to soften a brittle wife has failed, and because the image of Christ that has enlisted his moral allegiance is thought by Sarah Ruth to be blasphemous. Literally, it is blasphemous, and if the text is read on the level of psychological realism, then it is the story of a terrible mistake. But the difficulty of seeing the tattoo as only a tattoo, the strain of finding even thin psychological motivation that is sound, suggests that there is more to the story than marital strife. In fact, the incongruity between the comic gesture to please Sarah Ruth and the weight of surrounding circumstances—the burning trees, the eerie light, the piercing eyes of the Byzantine Christ—compels the search for a more contrived meaning to these strange events. In the end, a very simple device seems to be at work: O'Connor illustrates a man "getting religion" by effecting the "getting" literally. Christ is under the skin of Parker's back by virtue of a tattooist's needles. However, the conduct that follows is more fittingly the behavior of a man who has had a spiritual encounter with Christ rather than merely a physical alteration. Beyond this behavioral clue, there have been the revelations, the author's explanations at strategic points, and the exposure of consciousness at others to tell the audience in no uncertain way that O. E. Parker has met his God.

To the extent that "Parker's Back" is a contrived, obvious story, it is also an uncomfortable one to read. The postures of the author become distorted as she strains to make the action credible and at the same time representative of religious experience. O'Connor realized the awkwardness of her stance. "It's not necessary to point out that the look of this fiction is going to be wild, that it is almost of necessity going to be violent and comic, because of the discrepancies that it seeks to combine." But it is not to violence or comedy that the reader objects; rather it is to the sense of meaning being forced into the unwilling mold of unrelated events, of actions having to carry disproportionate moral weight. As soon as O'Connor's vision is made accessible through whatever means, it subjects itself to being judged. The problem of distance between an author and readers changes from a problem of cognition—whether the audience can recognize intended meanings—to the problem of consent. It is at this point that an unambiguous moral position in a work of art runs the risk of being rejected; a message offered at the expense of good craftsmanship can exceed the bounds of rhetorical manipulation that most dispassionate audiences are willing to accept.

A reason for the tendentious suggestion in "Parker's Back" has already been suggested. At the point of death, facing for herself the issue that had been of central concern to characters in her fiction, O'Connor must have wanted to make sure that people understood her. In her final hours, the risk of offending a hostile audience must have seemed small indeed.

IV

It seems appropriate to end, however, with a discussion not of O'Connor's last story but with one written in mid-career. She admitted that this tale, "The Artificial Nigger," was her favorite story. Subject to none of the cumbersome manipulation of "Parker's Back," it tells the story of common events in the lives of ordinary people, and manages nonetheless to make the experience of grace apparent.

Undoubtedly, it is one of her most engaging narratives, and it works on the anagogical as well as the literal level. During a symposium at Vanderbilt University in 1957 she explained the title.

> Well, I never had heard the phrase before, but my mother was out trying to buy a cow, and she rode up the country a-piece. She had the address of a man who was supposed to have a cow for sale, but she couldn't find it, so she stopped in a small town and asked the countryman on the side of the road where the house was, and he said, "Well, you go into this town and you can't miss it 'cause it's the only house in town with a artificial nigger in front of it." So I decided I would have to find a story to fit that. A little lower level than starting with the theme.

So the story began with an image, and O'Connor's imagination worked from this toward construction of a narrative that would reveal the importance of the black plaster lawn fixture. Her description of the starting point is very similar to Faulkner's explanation of the beginning of *The Sound and the Fury*. "It began with a mental picture. I didn't realize at the time it was symbolical. The picture was of the muddy seat of a little girl's drawers in a pear tree, where she could see through a window where her grandmother's funeral was taking place and report what was happening to her brothers on the ground below." Faulkner went on to discuss the process by which he recognized the implications of the picture of Caddy and translated it into narrative. Of a similar procedure in O'Connor's thinking, we have no record; but the mental route must have been devious, for the story begins very far from the middle-class lawns where such statuary is usually to be found in the South.

The story is simple in conception. Mr. Head, an old man bringing up his only grandson alone, decides to take the boy to the city for the first time. The trip, designed to teach "a lesson that the boy would never forget," is a disaster, for Mr. Head gets lost and barely succeeds in catching the last train home. The sojourn in the city is, in effect, a descent into hell for both of them; they spend hours bleakly confronting their own ignorance and, finally, their alienation from each other. In establishing the isolation and disgrace that overcome these two, in portraying their loss of innocence, O'Connor is masterful, for it is the depth of this domestic despair that measures the joyousness of their final reunion. Unlike many situations in the O'Connor canon, "The Artificial Nigger" ends with the release of tension and the reestablishment of trust.

The pivotal event in the story is Mr. Head's denial of Nelson. Young and eager to convince his grandfather of his independence, the boy had annoyed the old man with the reminder that he had been born in the city and that he was, in fact, returning to it. To Mr. Head, this is nonsense; he wants the boy to recognize the vanity of city life and, conversely, to understand his own will and strong character.

Although the old man does not realize it, this process begins almost as soon as the journey gets underway. There had been a long-standing dispute about whether the child would recognize a Negro if he saw one; he doesn't. Nelson moves to leave the train at the wrong station; Mr. Head corrects him. O'Connor tells her readers what the grandfather is too self-absorbed to recognize, that "for the first time in his life, he [Nelson] understood that his grandfather was indispensable to him." With this comment, O'Connor lays the foundation for the dramatic irony that follows, for Mr. Head remains bent on proving what the readers already know to be unnecessary. Nelson's discomfort and recognition of dependence have begun before he sets foot in this unnamed city. What follows, then, as the old man tries to further the boy's education, is seen to be gratuitously cruel. At the boy's moments of greatest vulnerability, the old man deserts him:

first, he hides when the boy wakes from an exhausted nap; then, when the child has upset a woman's groceries by his panicked response to solitude, Mr. Head denies his kinship: "This is not my boy . . . I never seen him before."

In the remainder of the story, O'Connor leads her audience as Mr. Head had never been able to lead young Nelson. She indicates the spiritual dilemma of both man and boy in ways that would not have occurred to them, in language beyond their command. Nelson becomes a mute zombie, unreachable by the normal human gestures of reconciliation. Silent and disconsolate, he drags behind Mr. Head, who experiences increasingly the horror of his denial. The author enters the mind of her character, not only revealing but reformulating the emotions that surface therein. Mr. Head wants to fall into the sewers and be swept away in the disgusting elements that mirror his soul; he sees his future as a hollow tunnel; he knows that he is "wandering into a black strange place where nothing was like it had ever been before, a long old age without respect and an end that would be welcome because it would be the end." This inner malaise is so relentlessly disclosed that when the old man calls to a fat suburbanite in bermuda shorts "Oh Gawd, I'm lost!," his cry expresses a despairing displacement of soul, even though the fat man responds, as he should, with directions to the nearest train station.

We are told, though, that physical relocation is not an answer, for the child has not recovered from his desertion; in a sense he has no home to return to. It is at this point that O'Connor intercedes, exposing the artificial nigger, the motivating image of her story, in a context that is heavy with latent emotion. The old man and boy stand amazed before this chipped piece of statuary, and O'Connor tells us exactly what they experience.

> They stood gazing at the artificial Negro as if they were faced with some great mystery, some monument to another's victory that brought them together in their common defeat. They could both feel it dissolving their differences like an action of mercy. Mr. Head had never known before what mercy felt like because he had been too good to deserve any, but he felt he knew now. He looked at Nelson and understood that he must say something to the child to show that he was still wise and in the look the boy returned he saw a hungry need for that assurance. Nelson's eyes seemed to implore him to explain once and for all the mystery of existence.

> Mr. Head opened his lips to make a lofty statement and heard himself say, "They ain't got enough real ones here. They got to have an artificial one."

It is an object as strange to Nelson and Mr. Head as it was initially to O'Connor that bridges the spiritual alienation of the man and boy. There is no aura of portentous allusion surrounding the object; it does not represent anything other than itself. But it functions uniquely in the lives of the protagonists, enabling them to forgive and be forgiven. In some ways, the scene is similar to the mental encounters Franz Kafka described in his letters to Felice Bauer. "For a long time now I have planned . . . to cut out and collect from various papers news items that astonished me for some reason, that affected me, that seemed . . . to be meant only for me." In the same way that the news items were public but of very particular, private interest to Kafka, the statue is open for anyone to see; but it is especially important to Mr. Head and Nelson. To reinforce the sense of releasing insight, O'Connor exposes Mr. Head's musings a second time.

> Mr. Head stood very still and felt the action of mercy touch him again but this time he knew that there were no words in the world that could name it. He understood that it grew out of agony, which is not denied to any man and which is given in strange ways to children. He understood it was all a man could carry into death to give his Maker. . . . He stood appalled, judging himself with the thoroughness of God, while the action of mercy covered his pride like a flame and consumed it.

The meaning of the encounter is unambiguously rendered. Nothing is left hidden. With the disclosure of Mr. Head's thoughts, the author has revealed her own understanding as well. The reader is not left to surmise an extraordinary significance for the statue, in the way he was left to assign portentous meanings to the bull in "Greenleaf." He is told straightforwardly that the statue has evoked a religious experience and that Mr. Head's epiphany occurs in the terms of traditional Christian theology. It is the Christian God who has spoken to him, and the old man interprets his own character and situation in light of Original Sin, damnation, and release from suffering. O'Connor's willingness to assume the full privilege of omniscient author has carried her through this passage cleanly and without the heavy ambiguities that often linger in other scenes of supposed revelation. There is no room for a reader's misinterpretation here, for as so infrequently happens in O'Connor's work, nothing is left to inference.

I would suggest that in these times of moral relativity, at an historical moment when no communal values can guide the assignment of anagogical meanings in fiction, this is the most effective and ultimately the most graceful narrative approach for the writer of religious concern. For a statement of faith is easier for an agnostic reader to accept than O'Connor's usual tendency toward oblique insult, which ensues from the intimation that her fictional world is fraught with portentous meanings that we could see if only we were not such monstrous readers, and too limited to understand.

RONALD SCHLEIFER

Rural Gothic

There are two qualities that make fiction. One is the sense of mystery and the other is the sense of manners. You get manners from the texture of existence that surrounds you. The great advantage of being a Southern writer is that we don't have to go anywhere to look for manners. . . . We in the South live in a society that is rich in contradiction, rich in irony, rich in contrast, and particularly rich in speech.

In *A Portrait of the Artist,* that most ungothic of literary works, Stephen Dedalus explains to his friend Lynch that although Aristotle had not defined pity and terror in the *Poetics,* he, Stephen, had:

> Pity is the feeling which arrests the mind in the presence of whatsoever is grave and constant in human sufferings and unites it with the human sufferer. Terror is the feeling which arrests the mind in the presence of whatsoever is grave and constant in human sufferings and unites it with the secret cause.

Stephen is attempting to define tragic art, yet his definitions are useful in developing a sense of the larger movements of Gothic fiction — of the serious contemplation of the supernatural in literature. The novel, I would argue, seeks to achieve some sense of Stephen's "pity," to create the texture of a social world in which we can join in sympathy with its human sufferers. What has characterized the great novelists in English — from Defoe through Fielding and George Eliot

From *Modern Fiction Studies* 28, no. 3 (Autumn 1982). © 1982 by the Purdue Research Foundation, West Lafayette, Ind. Originally entitled "Rural Gothic: The Stories of Flannery O'Connor."

to the human comedy of *Ulysses* itself—is an abiding sense of sympathy for the human sufferer, or its opposite, a sense of irony toward him. Another way to say this is to argue that the novel seeks to hide and to erase its own origins, to present itself and its characters on their own terms within the context of "the texture of existence that surrounds" them [*Mystery and Manners;* all further references to this text will be abbreviated as *MM*], whereas the Gothic romance seeks to reveal its hidden origins. The novel deals with the middle between apocalyptic ends; it deals with ongoing life, with what William Spanos, following Kierkegaard, calls the "interesting," "the intentionality of *inter esse* 'meaning (i) "to be between," (ii) "to be a matter of concern." ' "

The Gothic romance, on the other hand, seeks extremes; it proceeds, as Peter Brooks has noted, by means of the logic of the excluded middle. "It is not made from the mean average or the typical," Flannery O'Connor has written, "but from the hidden and often the most extreme" (*MM*); "it is the extreme situation that best reveals what we are essentially" (*MM*). The Gothic romance, when it is serious, seeks essences; it seeks origins—both its own and its characters'. That is, it seeks Joyce's "secret cause" and achieves, in the course of that quest, the terror Stephen talks of. Origins are always supernatural; they are always beyond what can be known in a rational, logical way. That is why Stephen talks of the "mystical estate" of fatherhood as the basis of the Catholic Church in *Ulysses,* because "it is founded, like the world, macro- and microcosm, upon the void." Origins are always what O'Connor calls "mystery," the manifestation and apprehension of the Sacred within quotidian reality. The Gothic tradition arose, Brooks argues, "at the dead end of the Age of Reason, [when] the Sacred reasserted its claim to attention, but in the most primitive possible manifestations, as taboo and interdiction. . . . [The Gothic tradition] reasserts the presence in the world of forces which cannot be accounted for by the daylight self and the self-sufficient mind." The daylight self and the self-sufficient mind are inhabitants of novels, where union with the human sufferer is enough and supernatural origins are beside the point: we need not know Moll Flanders' real parentage and name to feel the sympathetic understanding she occasions; and although Tom Jones's parentage is of some importance, it is precisely his indifference to such questions that makes him so appealing.

The Gothic novel, however, presents precisely the need to discover origins: its characters, from *The Castle of Otranto* on, seek to find (or find thrust upon themselves) their parentage and their origins. The Gothic is a haunted literature (it is no accident that both Joyce and O'Connor come from a Catholic tradition that takes the presence of the supernatural seriously), and what haunts it—whether it be Count Dracula, the Frankenstein monster, or the governess' ghosts in *The Turn of the Screw*—is some supernatural origin, some inhuman silence, forces beyond the self-sufficiency of the daylight self. These forces raise the question of identity and origin for the characters of Gothic romance: "who and what am I?" ask Frankenstein's monster and Lewis' Monk and Kafka's K.; "how can I discover those forces beyond myself that originate myself, my own 'secret cause'?" To put these questions in literary terms especially appropriate to Flannery O'Connor, how can we discover the origins of the power of literature, the originary force of metaphorical language? Such discoveries, as Stephen suggests, are made in terror, made in the loss of self within its secret cause. "To know oneself," O'Connor has written, "is, above all, to know what one lacks" (*MM*): it is a way of exploring the self and the world in a manner different from sympathetic understanding, through terror, violence, and encounter with the supernatural. O'Connor goes on to say,

> St. Cyril of Jerusalem, in instructing catechumens, wrote: "The dragon sits by the side of the road, watching those who pass. Beware lest he devour you. We go to the Father of Souls, but it is necessary to pass the dragon." No matter what form the dragon may take, it is of this mysterious passage past him, or into his jaws, that stories of any depth will always be concerned to tell, and this being the case, it requires considerable courage at any time, in any country, not to turn away from the storyteller.
>
> (*MM*)

Seeking the Father of Souls — the secret cause and origin of identity and the "rich speech" that manifests identity — the writer and the reader must pass the dragon outside; they must, as O'Connor continually insists, recognize the literal reality of the devil, the poverty of our self-sufficiency, and the necessity of grace. Such self-knowledge is a form of agony; as O'Connor says in what I believe is her best story, "The Artificial Nigger" — a story whose plot literally repeats the plot of St. Cyril's parable, with the artificial nigger a silent figure on the side of the road — such knowledge grows "out of agony, which is not denied to any man and which is given in strange ways to children." [*The Complete Stories of Flannery O'Connor;* all further references to this text will be abbreviated as *CS*]. It is this "mysterious passage" that the Gothic tradition offers us when it is most serious, a passage to and through origin and identity to their secret cause.

Nowhere are origins and identity such pressing problems, as Roy Male has recently shown, than on the frontier, where one continually encounters "mysterious strangers" who raise questions about one's own as well as others' identity. One such modern frontier is O'Connor's South: it is especially a "frontier" for a Catholic writer in the predominantly fundamentalist Protestant South. Like the Gothic romance Brooks describes, O'Connor seeks in her work to "reassert" the Sacred in the quotidian world, to situate her characters on the mysterious passage between the "manners" of novels and the "mystery" of union with secret causes. Tvzetan Todorov's study, *The Fantastic,* situates Gothic fiction on the "frontier" between natural and supernatural understandings of experience. In fact, although he does not use it, "frontier" itself is an apt metaphor for the situation of the Gothic as Todorov defines it: "the fantastic is that hesitation experienced by a person who knows only the laws of nature, confronting an apparently supernatural event." This is O'Connor's "frontier," that of a fiction which is always

> pushing its own limits outward towards the limits of mystery, because . . . the meaning of a story does not begin except at a depth where adequate motivation and adequate psychology and the various determinations have been exhausted. Such a writer . . . will be interested in possibility rather than probability. He will be interested in characters who are forced out to meet evil and grace and who act on a trust beyond themselves.
>
> (*MM*)

The Gothic, that is, presents a world beyond the understandings of metaphor, a world of mysterious inhuman forces that cannot adequately be explained by the metaphors of psychology or sociology or well-meaning humanism. It is a literature of *presence* unmediated by the substitutions of language, presences which are inhuman, terrifying, *secret.*

Yet O'Connor's frontier is more literal than this: her constant gesture is to place her characters between the natural and the supernatural by locating them, often on a literal journey, between the cities and the rural country of the South. "What the Southern Catholic writer is apt to find, when he descends within his imagination," she notes, "is not Catholic life but the life of this region in which he is both native and alien" (*MM*). Rufus Johnson in "The Lame Shall Enter First"—a character who embodies, as many of O'Connor's characters do, the *reality* of the devil—has a history of "senseless destruction, windows smashed, city trash boxes set afire, tires slashed—the kind of thing . . . found where boys had been transplanted abruptly from the country to the city as this one had" (*CS*). This is where the supernatural is most clearly and terrifyingly encountered—on those frontiers between the country and the city, faith and faithlessness, Protestant fundamentalism and cosmopolitan skepticism. Yet Rufus Johnson, as the well-meaning humanist-protagonist of the story learns, cannot be explained: he is simply a literal force, the force of the devil, to be encountered on this "frontier." "I have found," O'Connor writes, "that anything that comes out of the South is going to be called grotesque by the Northern reader" (*MM*), and she found this because the *strangeness* of that frontier in our culture—that location of the clashes between terror and pity—forces upon her characters confrontations with themselves and origins beyond themselves. "While the South is hardly Christ-centered," O'Connor says, "it is most certainly Christ-haunted" (*MM*).

II

"The problem of the novelist who wishes to write about a man's encounter with this God," O'Connor has written, "is how he shall make the experience — which is both natural and supernatural—understandable, and credible, to his reader" (*MM*). This is O'Connor's literary problem, to make the Sacred literal in a world in which it seems at best metaphorical, originating in a mode of perception rather than in the created world. Her problem, then, is the problem of the Gothic. Perhaps the best place to see her struggling with the problem is in one of her less successful stories, one that comes close to parodying the more powerful expressions of her repeated theme and plot, "An Enduring Chill." This story relates the return to rural Georgia from New York of Asbury Fox. Asbury, a twenty-five-year-old man, had gone to New York to become a literary artist, but now he is returning home to his mother without having written anything because he finds himself dying. Asbury is one of the characters in O'Connor's work—Hulga in "Good Country People," Julien in "Everything That Rises," Calhoun in "The Partridge Festival" are others—who has come to believe in nothing but himself and his own powers of perception. He, like the others, wants to teach his mother a lesson before he dies, to teach her of a realm beyond what he calls "her literal mind" of larger, sophisticated, metaphorical values. Thus on earlier visits home he had smoked and drunk warm milk with the Negro workers in his mother's dairy farm in order to shock her out of her complacencies. His mother, like so many other characters in O'Connor, lives in a self-satisfied, cliché-ridden world, a world where the metaphors of cliché are never examined at all. Asbury, like Hulga and Julien, participates in the egocentric life of his mother even while he is unaware of it: his mode of shocking her is to face her with the reality of his own dying, to counter her mindless optimism with his own brand of mindless, melodramatic pessimism. He wants her to understand the meaning — the metaphorical significance — of his death. To open her eyes he has left her a letter to be opened after his approaching death:

If reading it would be painful to her, writing it had sometimes been unbearable to him — for in order to face her, he had had to face himself. "I came here to escape the slave's atmosphere of home," he had written, "to find freedom, to liberate my imagination, to take it like a hawk from its cage and set it 'whirling off into the widening gyre' (Yeats) and what did I find? It was incapable of flight. It was some bird you had domesticated, sitting huffy in its pen, refusing to come out!" The next words were underscored twice. "I have no imagination. I have no talent. I can't create. I have nothing but the desire for these things. Why didn't you kill that too? Woman, why did you pinion me?"

(CS)

Asbury's language, with its incessant "I's," is as egocentric as that of any character in O'Connor's stories. He fails to "face himself" in his letter because he himself is simply a cliché — of a writer and a son. He can only speak of himself in the tired metaphors of "freedom" and "birds," and his "desires" are projections of himself rather than desires for things in the world. He even misquotes Yeats in order to humanize Yeats's metaphor for the presence of inhuman powers and to make it the narrated description of his own imagination.

Nevertheless, the act of "facing oneself" is the recurrent action of O'Connor's stories, the action of Gothic romance. Perhaps the most striking example of this is that of O. E. Parker in "Parker's Back," who literally "faces" his own back with a giant tattoo of Jesus, the eyes of which "continued to look at him — still, straight, all-demanding, enclosed in silence" (CS). This is a representative Gothic gesture: to make the metaphorical literal. Gothic romance does this, as Todorov and others have shown, by narrating dream and nightmare as reality and projecting our deepest impulses and fears onto the landscape. The face on Parker's back — its "all-demanding" eyes — made Parker feel "that his dissatisfaction was gone, but he felt not quite like himself. It was as if he were himself but a stranger to himself, driving into a new country though everything he saw was familiar to him, even the night" (CS). Such a feeling — a feeling that the reader is never sure Asbury achieves or not, hence the relative failure of "An Enduring Chill" — is what Freud calls the "uncanny," "that class of terrifying which leads back to something long known to us, once very familiar"; "the uncanny," Freud says, "would always be that in which one does not know where one is, as it were." The uncanny is familiar and strange, just as Parker is both familiar and strange to himself with God's constant eyes literally *upon* him, and he is in a country in which he is both native and alien.

That country is the country of the frontier, between the familiar and strange, the natural and supernatural. One gets there in O'Connor by "facing" oneself, by seeking origins and seeing oneself, as Mr. Head does, with God's own eyes, with God's eyes *upon* one. The Gothic, I have said, makes the metaphorical literal, and in this action we can see why O'Connor's backwoods' characters so often use country clichés in their speech: her act is to make us see the familiar as strange, to make us see literally and thus strangely what we usually don't see at all because it is so familiar. "Christ!" someone says in the pool hall when Parker reveals his tattoo (*CS*), and suddenly—almost supernaturally—O'Connor creates Christ's presence, as literal as it is for Parker, by means of the cliché of astonishment. In "The River," Bevel learns of Jesus:

> He had found out this morning that he had been made by a carpenter named Jesus Christ. Before he had thought it had been a doctor named Sladewell, a fat man with a yellow mustache who gave him shots and thought his name was Herbert. . . . If he had thought about it before, he would have thought Jesus Christ was a word like "oh" or "damn" or "God," or maybe somebody who had cheated him out of something sometime.
>
> (*CS*)

Such a discovery is the terrifying revelation of what we already knew: "carpenter" in this context takes on the full presence of its literal meaning of a maker, and Bevel (something a carpenter makes) is faced with the terrifying prospect of seeing himself anew.

Such confrontations with the literal—the literal self, its literal origin, a literal meaning—are the repeated actions in Flannery O'Connor, and they take place in what John Hawkes has called "her almost luridly bright pastoral world," on borderlines between the city and the country or between day and night. This is why so often O'Connor's stories end at sunset, as in "Revelation," when Mrs. Turpin watches her hogs as the sun goes down:

> Then like a monumental statue coming to life, she bent her head slowly and gazed, as if through the very heat of mystery, down into the pig parlour at the hogs. They had settled all in one corner around the old sow who was grunting softly. A red glow suffused them. They appeared to pant with a secret life.
>
> (*CS*)

From this sight she looks up as the sun goes down and sees her vision of a vast hoard of souls going to heaven, "whole companies of white trash, clean for the first time in their lives, and bands of black niggers in white robes, and battalions of freaks and lunatics shouting and clapping and leaping like frogs" (*CS*). The metaphor O'Connor uses is almost an allusion to *Otranto* with its giant statue coming to life, but the language is that of Mrs. Turpin, another in O'Connor's procession of good country people. That language informs a rural vision,

Hawkes's lurid pastoral world, with a sense of supernatural force so that the whole is seen in a new light. Here again O'Connor creates the *presence* of the supernatural, of mysterious forces beyond the daylight self, in pig and sunset. "Revelation" begins with Mrs. Turpin's confrontation with a Wellesley student in a doctor's office, yet it ends with her own uncouthness—her own rural sensibility—miraculously transformed in the presence of a secret life.

That life is Mrs. Turpin's life, but dark, unknown, strange: it is the life revealed in the college girl's fierce remark: "Go back to hell where you came from, you old wart hog" (*CS*). It is the inhuman life of wart hogs from hell that, literalized, leads strangely to Mrs. Turpin's vision of heaven. Mrs. Turpin "faces" herself with the hog; she sees her own secret life in the elemental life of her farm and discovers, as Parker had, the presence of God in and beyond His creation, in and beyond the hogs, the people, the peculiar light of the setting sun.

This is the light of grace, and it appears again at another sunset situated between the city and the country at the end of "The Artificial Nigger." There Mr. Head and his grandson, Nelson, after the small Inferno of their day in Atlanta, discover in the accidental image of suffering in a delapidated statue of a Negro the "action of mercy." What is powerful in O'Connor is her ability to create the *presence* of Christ and grace felt through and beyond the world of nature. How she does this is the problem and the secret of her art, and it is an art that is Gothic and that depends, fully, on its situation on one of the frontiers of our culture. Herman Melville wrote in *The Confidence-Man,* "it is with fiction as with religion: it should present another world, and yet one to which we feel the tie." O'Connor, like Melville, presents another world of white trash, black niggers, freaks, lunatics—in a word, a world of "good country people"—which is tied to ours yet strangely literal in its very landscape and language. That tie with our world is the tie with what she calls the "action of mercy," and in her best work it is "tied" through her metaphoric language becoming literal. Love is the burden of "The Artificial Nigger": face to face with a broken-down statue of a Negro, Mr. Head and his grandson are "faced with some great mystery, some monument to another's victory that brought them together in their common defeat" so that they "both feel it dissolving their differences *like an action of mercy*" (*CS*). This encounter creates a sense of humility for Mr. Head until, three paragraphs later, "he stood appalled . . . while *the action of mercy* covered his pride like a flame and consumed it." In the course of these paragraphs (and in the course of Mr. Head's experience), simile is rendered as assertion until, before our eyes, grace manifests itself, the action of mercy, the secret cause, appears:

> [Mr. Head] stood appalled, judging himself with the thoroughness
> of God, while the action of mercy covered his pride like a flame and

consumed it. He had never thought himself a great sinner before but he saw now that his true depravity had been hidden from him lest it cause him despair. He realized that he was forgiven for sins from the beginning of time, when he had conceived in his own heart the sin of Adam, until the present when he had denied poor Nelson. He saw that no sin was too monstrous for him to claim as his own, and since God loved in proportion as He forgave, he felt ready at that instance to enter Paradise.

(CS)

This is the "secret cause" that Joyce speaks of, a sense of God's presence and love in the heart of Mr. Head. But what is remarkable about this passage, I believe, is that we never question the fact that the realization described — its language and its theology — is simply beyond the frontier language and evangelical Christianity of Mr. Head. (Head, hick that he is, believes that an inferno underlies Atlanta and fears to be sucked down the sewer: he literalizes his own metaphor — see *CS*.) What reveals itself here is grace, and like the Mormon's magical glasses, grace includes the ability to see and to understand another language.

This language is that of sympathy: the passage suggests that Head can only understand the "secret cause" — here the sin of Adam — by experiencing the agony of his own egocentric denial of "poor Nelson." Mr. Head is not truly a part of the world he lives in — neither is Mrs. Turpin, O. E. Parker, Asbury Fox, and most of O'Connor's protagonists — and his struggle, like that of the others and like our own, is to find some connection in a world that simply seems alien, other, without human response. It is a world, as the Misfit says in "A Good Man is Hard to Find," in which, without an answering Jesus, there's no pleasure but meanness, "no real pleasure in life" (*CS*) — a world in which, as O'Connor says, we are native and alien. How to discover a human response in such a world is the great problem: Mr. Head can, as he has done all his life, depend on himself and his ability to give "lessons" and be a "suitable guide for the young" (*CS*), or he can discover, in terror or in love, but above all in humility, supernatural forces outside himself that lead him to other human sufferers who can respond to himself. Most of O'Connor's heroes fall into terror: they find, as Parker does, the terrifying cost of God's enduring eye; or they find, as the Misfit does, the senselessness of not knowing God is there. As O'Connor herself says, "Often the nature of grace can be made plain only by describing its absence" (*MM*), and such absence *is* inhuman; it leaves our world literally senseless and results in the senseless violence — the inhuman violence — of all those who do not fit: the Misfit, Rufus, Shiftlet, and all the rest. But others — Mrs. Turpin, Mr. Head, Bailey's mother — discover love amid their terror: they discover the literal language of

God already in their own Southern slang. They achieve humility when they realize that they are not fully self-possessed, that their "calm understanding," as it is said of Head, leaves out their own mysterious origins and forces beyond themselves. "An artificial nigger!" Mr. Head said to Nelson: "They ain't got enough real ones here. They got to have an artificial one" (*CS*). Face to face with suffering—face to face with himself—Head recognizes forces outside himself.

What the action of mercy finally does is offer a sense of grace, a sense of the supernatural, in the world in which O'Connor characters, both native and alien, do not quite fit. "An Enduring Chill" is a parody of the kind of story—the Gothic romance—O'Connor writes. In the end we discover Asbury is not dying at all, despite all his histrionics: he had simply poisoned himself with the unpasteurized milk he had drunk during his last visit. But meanwhile, much as Tanner orchestrates his own funeral in "Judgement Day," imagining himself shipped home to Georgia from New York in his casket out of which he would jump on his arrival, shouting: "Judgement Day! Judgement Day! . . . Don't you two fools know it is Judgement Day?" (*CS*), so Asbury orchestrates his own end. He calls for a Catholic priest, hoping to engage him in a literary debate, only to find the priest is as ignorant as his mother; he insults the family doctor; and he calls the household Negroes to his deathbed for a touching farewell. In the end, however, he learns he is not going to die, and, as he lies in bed at the end of the story with his nonfatal fever, he looks at a discoloration on the ceiling of his room that had always reminded him of a bird.

> The boy fell back on his pillow and stared at the ceiling. His limbs that had been racked for so many weeks by fever and chill were numb now. The old life in him was exhausted. He awaited the coming of the new. It was then that he felt the beginning of a chill, a chill so peculiar, so light, that it was like a warm ripple across a deeper sea of cold. His breath came short. The fierce bird which through the years of his childhood and the days of his illness had been poised over his head, waiting mysteriously, appeared all at once to be in motion. Asbury blanched and the last film of illusion was torn as if by a whirlwind from his eyes. He saw that for the rest of his days, frail, racked, but enduring, he would live in the face of a purifying terror. A feeble cry, a last impossible protest escaped him. But the Holy Ghost, emblazoned in ice instead of fire, continued, implacable, to descend.
>
> (*CS*)

This is a far cry from the "action of mercy" in "The Artificial Nigger": here nothing appears in this story of a pseudo-sophisticated, spiteful boy to prepare for this supernatural intervention. Yet it is precisely because "An Enduring Chill" ends so abruptly that we can trace the "action" of grace in the story. Grace is occasioned by its own absence, by the despair, leading to rage or to humility, that all of O'Connor's characters, saved or not, fall into. Rage is always present, always seemingly a supernatural force. Humility translates this Gothic rage into rage against the daylight self and the self-sufficient mind to allow the apprehension not of projections of self but of the self itself, originating elsewhere. That is, to quote Yeats (correctly this time), "Where there is nothing—there is God." The grandmother in "A Good Man is Hard to Find" finally sees, literally, that she is responsible for the Misfit *because* God literally loves her, despite the apparent terrible, murderous, absence of love; she sees that her clichés about Jesus are literally true, even though she has used them throughout the story when she had nothing to say. "The Enduring Chill" does not create the sense of the presence of God, I think, because its transformation from the metaphoric absence of grace to the literal presence of the Holy Ghost is not convincing: Asbury's "defeat" does not fully succeed, and his vision, unlike that of Mrs. Turpin and the grandmother, isn't grounded in his own backwoods belief.

What the rural Southern frontier finally offers O'Connor is that position in the world—that situation—where the strangers you meet can be anyone, can, in fact, be supernatural: Jesus, the devil, the Holy Ghost.

> "I can tell you my name is Tom S. Shiftlet and I come from Tarwater, Tennessee, but you never have seen me before: how you know I ain't lying? How you know my name ain't Aaron Sparks, lady, and I come from Singleberry, Georgia, or how you know it's not George Speeds and I come from Lucy, Alabama, or how you know I ain't Thompson Bright from Toolafalls, Mississippi?"
>
> (*CS*)

All these names, as Roy Male has suggested, are filled with light, and they set forth the action—sometimes the failed action—of O'Connor's Gothic fiction: to discover or create light out of the dark frontier of rural Georgia. "I think," O'Connor wrote, "[the Catholic writer] will feel a good deal more kinship with backwoods prophets and shouting fundamentalists than he will with those politer elements for whom the supernatural is an embarrassment of sociology or culture or personality development" (*MM*). That sense of supernatural force that the backwoods prophets feel in the world repeats itself in the uncanny force and presence O'Connor achieves within the cliché-ridden language of her fiction. Both acknowledge the supernatural and discover that it can be found on the edges of our culture, dark and empty as they may be, on the rural frontier.

FREDERICK ASALS

The Double

Conflict, often violent conflict, is at the very center of Flannery O'Connor's
fiction. Characters mutter, snarl, and rage at one another until the rising pressure of the action forces a climactic clash, a bursting of tensions often both
physical and deadly. Yet those same angry figures are viewed from a comic distance so severe that they hover on the edge of—and sometimes fall over into—
caricature. O'Connor's people are among the least introspective in modern fiction, with minds at once so unaware and so absurdly assured that they have
refused to acknowledge any deeper self. None of them are interested in what one
character calls his "underhead," and the result is the very fury of their responses,
for the unconscious exists in O'Connor's fiction not as a psychic area to be
probed but as a violent force denied. The ironic upshot of their denial is that her
characters thereby become obsessive figures, clinging in outrage to their narrowly rigid self-definitions in the face of all challenges. Incapable of doubt or
self-questioning, her protagonists are incapable of the flexibility of development, and the climaxes of the stories confront them with the startling image of
all they have denied. Their eyes are finally "shocked clean," but the shock is
sometimes sufficient to kill them as well.

As the screw of the action turns and tensions rise, again and again there appears before those self-denying characters a creature both strange and yet in
some way familiar, like a distorting mirror whose image they at once repudiate
but cannot quite turn away from—in short, a double figure. An expression in
character and action of O'Connor's characteristic duality, the pattern recurs so
often that it can only be called obsessive. Albert J. Guerard has justly remarked

From *Flannery O'Connor: The Imagination of Extremity.* © 1982 by the University of
Georgia Press.

that "the word *double* is embarrassingly vague as used in literary criticism," but in her work the configuration always takes one of two classic forms. Either one character discovers that another is a replica of himself, an almost identical reflection — here the paradigm would be twins — or, much more often, one character is presented as the alter ego of another, the embodiment of qualities suppressed or ignored by the first, a mirror image or inverse reflection. Here the paradigm perhaps receives its best expression in the myth of the *Symposium* that for each of us there exists a complementary self to which we were once physically attached; Freud's observation that two dramatized figures may together constitute a complete personality is its psycholiterary counterpart. Yet whichever form the double takes, he signals a widening split within the protagonist and is felt as an opposing self. The sense of uncanniness that always marks his appearance is sometimes muted in O'Connor, for since most of her works focus on relationships within a family the double figure may retain a surface plausibility. But the dismaying discovery of unwanted kinship can extend well beyond the family, and in fact beyond the human world altogether.

The heroes of both of the novels are deeply split within themselves. Almost inevitably, it seems, they also encounter everywhere doppelgängers who reflect aspects of their self-division. In the more compressed form of the story the central figures may not be so obviously dramatized as internally divided, but they are nevertheless forced again and again to gaze into an appalling mirror. Language and imagery heralding the doppelgänger abounds. "That was your black double" the son of "Everything That Rises Must Converge" archly confides to his dying mother, without considering the implications for himself; for if the large Negro woman of this story embodies a side of life his mother has refused to see, then to whom does her dependent little boy correspond? Old Mark Fortune of "A View of the Woods" complacently recognizes in his granddaughter a "small replica" of himself, a recognition that becomes intolerable when at the story's end "his own image" turns "triumphant and hostile." The only literal twins in O'Connor's fiction are the mysterious brothers of "Greenleaf," but it is no accident, as we shall see, that the protagonist of "The Comforts of Home" is called Thomas, a name which means "twin." From twins it is but a short step to brothers: near the beginning of "The Artificial Nigger," we recall, Mr. Head and Nelson "looked enough alike to be brothers and brothers not too far apart in age," and near the end of that story they stare at their saving alter ego, the little statue, in attitudes which are called "identical." In "Judgement Day" old Tanner gazes at the black exconvict Coleman and sees a "negative image of himself, as if clownishness and captivity had been their common lot." In "The Lame Shall Enter First" the social worker Sheppard discovers that Rufus Johnson's eyes have become "distorting mirrors in which he saw himself made hideous and grotesque."

Double, replica, twin, brother, negative image, mirror—this is the classic language of the doppelgänger motif. Of the traditional terms, only *shadow* seems to be missing; yet one recollects her comment on the apearance of the Negro in southern literature as "a figure for our darker selves, our shadow side," and certainly the image of the shadow is notably employed in both novels and in "The Artificial Nigger." While Hazel Motes strides through Taulkinham spewing forth blasphemies, he trails behind him "a thin nervous shadow walking backwards" (*Wise Blood*), and both Tarwater and the Heads discover "ghostlike" transparencies in train and store windows, shadowy selves that appear to have a being of their own. These last seem images of what Otto Rank called "the double as immortal self," a spiritual shadow that is deeply disturbing because it is part of a dimension not contained by the everyday world these characters prefer to think is all that exists.

But the double configuration need not appear only in these traditional ways. To take a minor (and undeveloped) example, O'Connor suggests it swiftly and subtly in the once-identical sunhats worn by Mrs. Cope and Mrs. Pritchard at the opening of "A Circle in the Fire." Mrs. Pritchard's is "faded and out of shape" while Mrs. Cope's is "still stiff and bright green," images which imply succinctly the opposed temperaments of the two women. Yet Mrs. Cope's frightened turning away from suffering and evil and Mrs. Pritchard's morbid delight in their graphic details are equally a denial of everything *sun* implies in this story, and different as the condition of the two hats is, they both serve to shield the women from its rays. Thus the hat image immediately adumbrates their roles as embodiments of a false polarity challenged by the appearance of the three boys. Similarly, in "The Partridge Festival" O'Connor surrounds both the protagonist, Calhoun, and his female counterpart, Mary Elizabeth, with echoing images of infantilism to suggest from the start what the characters themselves only reluctantly come to admit: that in childishly claiming they are "spiritual kin" to the criminal Singleton, "a kinship with each other was unavoidable." But in that immature assertion of kinship with the mad murderer, they discover—and it destroys their callow theorizing for good—there lurks an inescapable bond with the despised Partridge, the great world itself.

In such a story as "The Partridge Festival" the blending of the psychological and symbolic motif of the double with the social and cultural theme of kinship emerges clearly. Matters of kin are a natural enough subject for any southern writer, but, as has often been noted, O'Connor is especially preoccupied with the tensions and ambiguities of family relationships, particularly those between parent and child. The motif of kinship need not, however, be confined to blood ties. Perhaps the most poignant moment in *Wise Blood* is Hazel Motes's confession late in the novel, "My people are all dead," a remark that reverberates in the surrounding silence to reach beyond his lost family and touch on some more essential aloneness. And of course the best-known recognition scene in O'Connor's fiction is the grandmother's discovery in "A Good Man Is Hard to Find" that The Misfit is "one of [her] babies . . . one of [her] own children," a discovery that produces her instantaneous death, one senses, precisely because he feels it to be mysteriously true.

In the ominous and uncanny materialization of The Misfit out of the distant landscape, in the grandmother's "peculiar feeling" both that "she had known him all her life" and that "she could not recall who he was," and in that final recognition scene the shadow of the double motif seems to make itself felt. In any case, there is no difficulty in identifying it at work in "Revelation." Mrs. Turpin's comically furious cry, "How am I a hog and me both?" focuses her humbling discovery that her closest kin is not human at all, that her deepest nature denied in her fantasies of election and in her good works, is reflected in that old sow in her up-to-date pig parlor—and that however sanitized, a hog is a hog. But here as elsewhere in O'Connor the unveiling of true kinship is as self-estranging as it is self-revealing, for the climactic vision opens up to Mrs. Turpin a dimension in which even her virtues, which she had smugly taken for her deepest self, "were being burned away." Between the old sense of self and the new and dismaying knowledge, there opens a chasm hardly to be bridged.

Inherent in the very use of the double motif is a dualistic conception of the self, of character so deeply divided that an essential part can be embodied in an independent figure. That the configuration recurs throughout her fiction, as even this brief survey suggests, indicates how central to Flannery O'Connor's imagination it was. Yet the variety of changes she was able to ring on this basic construct is remarkable, and two somewhat more extended examples may help to give some sense of her inventiveness within an obsession. Here the stories which will serve, one from each of the collections she published, are precisely those glanced at in the previous chapter as illustrations of differing symbolic treatments of landscape: "A View of the Woods" and "Good Country People."

Although written later, "A View of the Woods" is the simpler (and the lesser) of these two works; it is also perhaps, of all O'Connor's stories, the one that most overtly makes use of the double motif. In her own terse words, "Mary Fortune and the old man [are] images of each other but opposite in the end" (*The Habit of Being*). For this metamorphosis of an apparent replica into a genuine alter ego, the pivot on which the action turns is the process of denial. Like a number of her other protagonists, seventy-nine-year-old Mark Fortune tries to reject the finality of his own death, in this case by "insur[ing] the future." Aware that the family over which he exercises an absolute despotism is "waiting impatiently for the day when they could put him in a hole eight feet deep and cover him up with dirt," he has attempted to perpetuate himself indefinitely in two ways. First, he has so dedicated himself to material progress that he expects the town being built mostly on his former property to be called Fortune, Georgia (his present project, in which a machine digs a hole out of the soft clay, is his symbolic resistance to that other and final hole). Second, he has trained his favorite granddaughter and heiress, Mary Fortune, to be in every way another edition of him. "A View of the Woods" presents what happens when these two schemes for self-perpetuation suddenly come into conflict.

The opening pages of the story repeatedly stress Mr. Fortune's awareness of the remarkable resemblance his granddaughter bears to him. Not only is she physically "a small replica of the old man," but "she was like him on the inside too. She had, to a singular degree, his intelligence, his strong will, and his push and drive." Despite the difference in their ages, "the spiritual distance between them was slight." All of this is a source of great satisfaction to the old man, who politely ignores the fact that Mary Fortune bears the family name Pitts and habitually speaks of the Pittses as if they are some tribe foreign to the two of them. "He liked to think of her," O'Connor writes, "as being thoroughly of his clay," made, presumably, of the same stuff as the rest of his property. And insofar as clay suggests his earth-bound vision, he seems to be right. Bearing "his unmistakable likeness," the child at first appears a precise copy of her grandfather, a clone that has unaccountably skipped a generation.

But it emerges that Mr. Fortune detects in her "one failure of character," which to him means "one point in which she did not resemble him." When her father summons Mary Fortune outside for a whipping, Mr. Fortune sees on her face a look "foreign" to it—a look, that is, that he cannot recognize as one he would be capable of—"part terror and part respect and part something else, something very like cooperation." When he berates the child for her submission, he cannot understand her ritualistic denial, "nobody's ever beaten me in my life and if anybody did, I'd kill him," although he dimly sees that these episodes are "Pitts's revenge on him," Pitts's indirect retaliation for the cruel power the old man holds over him. Nonetheless, this one flaw in an otherwise perfect child—perfect, of course, in her resemblance to him—remains for Mr. Fortune "an ugly mystery."

That flaw becomes the fissure that widens between them when Mary Fortune unexpectedly opposes his scheme to sell off the field in front of their house, a growing division in which the use of names, and thus of identity, is the central weapon. When early in the story the old man recalls the naming of the child Mary Fortune and refers to "the Pittses" as a group apart from "you and me," grandfather and granddaughter seem two versions of the same person, identical twins separated less by space and sex than by the time lapse of seventy years.

But as she stubbornly sets herself against the projected sale, he finds himself telling her, "You act more like a Pitts than a Fortune," his lowest insult and one he immediately regrets. Nevertheless, she perseveres in her resistance until he is driven to confront her:

> "Are you a Fortune," he said, "or are you a Pitts? Make up your mind."
> Her voice was loud and positive and belligerent.
> "I'm Mary — Fortune — Pitts," she said.
> "Well I," he shouted, "am PURE Fortune!"

The trumping of her claim to mixed identity is a challenge that she answers with physical violence, and when she momentarily bests him in their fight, as "pale identical eye looked into pale identical eye," she informs him, "You been whipped . . . by me . . . and I'm PURE Pitts." Enraged that "the face that was his own . . . had dared to call itself Pitts," with a surge of fury the old man crushes her head against a rock, saying, "There's not an ounce of Pitts in me."

It is an idle and self-defeating boast. Beneath the varieties of pride and family loyalty conveyed in the manipulations of these names, the very words themselves suggest irreconcilable values. *Fortune* proclaims the Faustian self — an identity dramatized in the old man's pact with the snakelike Tillman — the assertion of the egoistic seeker of power, self-inflating and self-aggrandizing, devotee of the ancient bitch-goddess of this world, projecting himself infinitely through time, "gorging" himself on earthly "clay." *Pitts,* however, expresses a knowledge that is biblical rather than Faustian: the Psalmist's pit of powerlessness and suffering, of pain, loss, and worldly defeat, from which opens an appalling glimpse of the bottomless pit and the inescapable awareness of that earthly pit to which we all go. Thus when Mary Fortune confronts her grandfather with his own image and labels it Pitts, the old man finds this alter ego intolerable precisely because, like The Misfit at the end of "A Good Man Is Hard to Find," he senses that it is true. It is Mr. Fortune, after all, who has had the momentary vision of the woods full of blood, wounds, and "hellish red trunks"; it is Mr. Fortune who has been so challenged by the child's opposition that he has repeatedly had to marshal his "principles" to carry on with the sale; it is Mr. Fortune whose unacknowledged terror of his own obliteration lies behind both his many property deals and his attempts to view the child as merely another edition of himself. And Mary Fortune has just given him a taste of the Pitts condition, attacking him "like a pack of small demons" until he "began to roll like a man on fire." No wonder "he seemed to see his own face coming to bite him," for the child here enacts not the replica of the worldly successful Fortune but the revolt of the buried self, the despised Pitts.

Paradoxically, at the moment she defeats him and identifies herself as "PURE Pitts," she has never been more Fortune-like in her position of power, while he has been forced into the subjugated posture of the humbled Pittses. But so unyielding is the old man's refusal to accept the Pitts within that he *must* reverse their roles, even at the expense of her life. "There's not an ounce of Pitts in me" is only the last of his many denials, the final rejection of a dimension of himself and of existence that his ravenous ego will not acknowledge. The battle has a wryly ironic upshot, for in his frenzy to erase the Pitts from his own identity, Mr. Fortune has not insured the future but destroyed it, thereby presumably delivering into the hands of the despised Pittses all his worldly clay. In devoting himself to the material kingdoms of the world—"the Whore of Babylon," Mary Fortune has humorously but pertinently called him—he has lost them all except the one impossible to escape, the pit where there squats his genuine replica, the mechanical "monster . . . as stationary as he was, gorging itself on clay."

"Good Country People" also presents a generational relationship within a family, in this case mother and daughter, but essential as that pairing is, it is not at the dramatic center of the story. The pivotal action is of course Joy-Hulga's encounter with the Bible salesman, a confrontation that focuses and ironically reflects the other relationships in the story, that between the two older women, Mrs. Hopewell and Mrs. Freeman, and those of the girl with each of them. For Mrs. Hopewell, life is apparently summed up in her stock of clichés, and the dialogues with Mrs. Freeman that begin the story are exercises in hackneyed one-upmanship:

> "Everybody is different," Mrs. Hopewell said.
> "Yes, most people is," Mrs. Freeman said.
> "It takes all kinds to make the world."
> "I always said it did myself."

Mrs. Hopewell's supply of platitudes runs to the general and the uplifting. On her outraged daughter she urges the virtues of a "pleasant expression," a "pleasant" manner, and such cheery advice as "a smile never hurt anyone," but to her bewildered dismay, the girl responds to none of this. "It seemed to Mrs. Hopewell that every year she grew less like other people and more like herself—bloated, rude and squint-eyed."

This evolution is of course precisely what her daughter intends. As in "A View of the Woods," naming again defines the shift: Joy's changing her name to Hulga is a deliberate defiance of her mother, a self-definition that sets her against everything Mrs. Hopewell stands for. "She saw it," O'Connor writes, "as the name of her highest creative act. One of her major triumphs was that her mother had not been able to turn her dust into Joy, but the greater one was that she had been able to turn it herself into Hulga." In this self-created rebirth, the girl believes, the ugly name acts as a mask for a private inner sense of identity: "She had a vision of the name working like the ugly sweating Vulcan who stayed in the furnace and to whom, presumably, the goddess [Venus] had to come when called." Cut off from the possibility of physical beauty by her "hulking" body and her wooden leg, Hulga emphasizes her outer ugliness in dress, manner, and action, but she secretly cherishes the vision of an inner self that is beautifully unique.

Forced by her physical disabilities to live at home, the girl's existence has become one continuous gesture of outraged rejection of the life around her. If her mother refuses to deal with anything but the genteel surfaces of life, Hulga scorns those surfaces and plunges into the "depths," acquiring a Ph.D. in philosophy and disdaining "any close attention to her surroundings." If Mrs. Hopewell approaches life with a naïve optimism, her daughter embraces atheistic nihilism, "see[ing] *through*" the surfaces of things "to nothing." Point by point, the girl has, she thinks, defined a self that is the antithesis of her mother's.

The mysterious appearance of the Bible salesman at the Hopewell home provides the first real test of that self called Hulga. As he presents himself, he seems a living embodiment of Mrs. Hopewell's most cherished clichés. "Honest," "sincere," "genuine," "simple," "earnest," "the salt of the earth," with his Bible-quoting and his missionary aspirations, he convinces the girl that at last she is "face to face with real innocence." Towards that innocence her feelings are deeply ambivalent. What she tells herself is that he is clay to be molded by her own "deeper understanding of life," an "inferior mind" to be instructed by "true genius," and she vaguely projects the aftermath of a seduction in which she transforms his inevitable remorse into "something useful." But what these fantasies of superiority reckon without is her unadmitted desire that someone pay homage to the goddess within.

The Bible salesman says that their meeting must have been fated "on account of what all [we] got in common," but all that they seem to have in common is a potentially fatal heart condition. Their apparent roles are a typical set of O'Connor antitheses—the academic and the country bumpkin, the sophisticate and the innocent, the cynical atheist and the naïve Christian—antitheses that reach their comic high point in the barn where, as the boy whines for a declaration of love, the girl gives him a crash course in nihilist epistemology. But in the sudden role reversal that takes place in that barn, we discover what a genuine doppelgänger this Bible salesman is.

The boy says of the wooden leg (which she treats "as someone else would his soul, in private and almost with her own eyes turned away"), "It's what makes you different. You ain't like anybody else." It is then that her outer cynicism drops and the girl reveals her underlying belief in real innocence: "This boy, with an instinct that came from beyond wisdom, had touched the truth about her." The shrine of the goddess has been approached at last and with an attitude apparently "entirely reverent." Her surrender to him is thus of more than her body, it is of her entire sense of self; and when she allows him to remove the leg, she becomes dependent on him for more than physical wholeness. Now he reveals to her who the true innocent is.

For the girl has not, as she thinks, escaped her mother and her mother's values: the entire identity of Hulga is built on them. Her academic nihilism is riddled with such clichés as "We are all damned . . . but some of us have taken off our blindfolds and see that there's nothing to see. It's a kind of salvation." If the language is more sophisticated than any at Mrs. Hopewell's command, it is no less trite, and the smug self-deception underlying it ("I don't have illusions") is, if anything, greater. Willfully blind to the world around her and complacent in her notion of self-created uniqueness, she has gained her sense of disdainful superiority precisely from her contemptuous acceptance of her mother's view of things. In kissing the boy, as we have seen, she falls into a parody of the maternal role, and when his childlike innocence becomes no longer credible, she asks, "Aren't you . . . aren't you just good country people?" The question is the ironic equivalent of Mrs. Hopewell's conviction that he is exactly that—a conviction her daughter has clearly shared.

As the mask of Hulga drops and reveals beneath it none other than Mrs. Hopewell's little girl Joy, it does so in response to the disappearance of the mask of the Bible salesman, of Manley Pointer, as he has called himself. And the face that looks forth from beneath *that* mask is the face of the nihilist the girl has claimed to be. She has pretended to be reborn into nothingness, but *he* has "been believing in nothing ever since I was born." Although we get only a glimpse of what lives beneath that mask—apparently, like The Misfit, the Bible salesman thrives on "meanness," in this case with a flair for the fetishistic—we see enough to grasp how uncannily mask and reality correspond to the Joy and Hulga identities of the girl. As the roles reverse themselves and his assumed innocence disappears into cynicism, so her superficial worldliness gives way to sentimental naïveté. If Manley Pointer turns out to be as hollow as the Bible he reveals in the barn, so Hulga is as empty as the wooden leg it was based on. "Like one presenting offerings at the shrine of a goddess," he takes from that Bible and places before her the contraceptives, whiskey, and pornographic cards that are a cruelly fitting devotion to the deified self. That self had been a sham; it is the girl, not the Bible salesman, who has the innocence of the child. Although he piously cites the text "He who losest his life shall find it," she is the one who truly believes in such a possibility, secularized though it is. For when she surrenders to him the privacy of the leg, "it was like losing her own life and finding it again, miraculously, in his." The text, of course, works here ironically: it is the precise formula for their exchange of apparent identities.

The climax of his role as mocking double comes in a vicious parody of the intellectual clichés the girl has earlier mouthed at him. Accused of hypocrisy, he replies indignantly, "I hope you don't think . . . that I believe in that crap! I may sell Bibles, but I know which end is up and I wasn't born yesterday and I know where I'm going!" But if the values here are the nihilistic ones the girl has professed, the idiom is the folk cliché so dear to Mrs. Hopewell, and the wedding of the two exposes with resonant finality how closely identified mother and daughter in truth are. Indeed, on this level "Good Country People" inverts the action of "A View of the Woods," for when Hulga is revealed as Joy, this apparent antithesis of her mother emerges as virtually a replica. The intricate set of reflections does not, however, end here, for the Bible salesman is not the only representative of those "good country people" in the story.

Mrs. Hopewell is of the opinion that Mrs. Freeman is also one of these "real genuine folks," and all the evidence ironically supports her. As Mrs. Freeman herself remarks, "Some people are more alike than others." Like the Bible salesman, she thrives on the exploitation of others' suffering—"Mrs. Freeman had a special fondness for the details of secret infections, hidden deformities, assaults upon children. Of diseases, she preferred the lingering or incurable"—and her persistent fascination with the girl's artificial leg is reflected and fulfilled in his successful theft of it. Even her "beady steel-pointed eyes" reappear at a higher pitch of intensity in his, "like two steel spikes" as they leer at the filched trophy. If Joy at last turns out to be truly her mother's daughter, so Mrs. Freeman emerges as a symbolic mother to the Bible salesman. And as he is given the last triumphant word in his duel with the girl, so Mrs. Freeman, characteristically pulling an "evil-smelling onion shoot" from the ground, has the final ironic word in the story: " 'Some can't be that simple' [as the Bible salesman appeared to be] she said, 'I know I never could.' "

The relationship between the two women which frames the central action thus turns out to be a less sinister version of the encounter between their real and symbolic children. Like her daughter, Mrs. Hopewell persuades herself that she is in control of the situation, and like her she is self-deceived, for it is Mrs. Freeman with her mechanical, "driving" gaze, her imperviousness, and her ability always to get the last word who dominates their relationship. If "Good Country People" does not quite present parallel plots—the central encounter becomes a dramatic reversal, the framing action remains static and ongoing—it does set before us four characters in interlocking reflective relationship, like facing mirrors slightly askew. The Bible salesman has the role of the classic double figure, but he is only the center of the set of images and identities that cast back mocking versions of one another. "Everybody is different," all agree, whether as folk banality or as the secret nourishing of the hidden self; but what the story dramatizes is how appallingly small and superficial those differences are. Some people are indeed more alike than others.

"A View of the Woods" and "Good Country People," then, employ the double motif in almost directly contrary ways. The former opens with the assertion that Mary Fortune Pitts is a replica of her grandfather and then gradually turns her into his alter ego, pure Pitts in deadly combat with pure Fortune. The latter story begins with Hulga as an antiself to her mother and then reveals the Joy hidden beneath, but it does so through an exchange of apparent identities between the girl and the doppelgänger of the Bible salesman, and further reflects *that* relationship in the comic mirror of Mrs. Hopewell and Mrs. Freeman's framing interchanges. Each story flashes at the protagonist a revelation of the unacknowledged self and thus hurls a decisive challenge at a cherished self-definition, but where one insists on differentiation, the other denies it. The effect on the protagonists cannot be other than shattering, but the difference between the disastrous ending of "A View of the Woods" and the comic climax of "Good Country People" is that between a refusal to recognize the double figure and the inability *not* to recognize him.

The differences here are genuine and important, yet underlying them is a pattern which is disturbingly characteristic of O'Connor's use of the double motif. The doppelgänger by definition creates a configuration of antitheses, of the acknowledged and the unacknowledged, of conscious and denied selves. But in O'Connor's tales this antithesis undergoes an intense pressure which drives it toward destruction; the result is a radical sundering which proclaims the failure of self-reconciliation. In both "A View of the Woods" and "Good Country People" what does not happen is underlined by its very inclusion, late in each story, as a momentary possibility. When, for instance, the child calls herself "Mary—Fortune—Pitts" she defines an integration of the warring selves designated by those names, but the story sweeps on to the mutual destruction of pure polarities. Analogously, Joy Hopewell's fantasy of "losing her life and finding it again, miraculously, in his" takes the practical form of "she would run away with him and . . . every night he would take the leg off and every morning put it back on again," an image of a kind of marriage in interdependence, a merging of the knowledge of Hulga with the innocence of Manley Pointer; but the action moves quickly to the girl's devastating defeat. In both works, of course, O'Connor has presented irreconcilable antagonists: between the attributes of Fortune and Pitts there is no point of meeting, and the only possible relationship between sentimental optimism and nihilistic hedonism is one of exploitation. Nevertheless, the child and the Bible salesman do embody denied sides of the self, the unrecognized Pitts and Joy within, and the failure—indeed, impossibility—of reconciliation in each story points once again to the extremity of O'Connor's imagination.

O'Connor's imagination seems usually to have begun its workings on a rather isolated, abrasive social context composed of the members of a family or the dwellers on a small farm, and then to have moved in one of two directions to bring about the dissolution or reordering of the original relationships. These two deeper movements, easily discernible beneath the variety of the surface actions of her stories, are versions of archetypal literary patterns hardly peculiar to O'Connor, but striking in the almost obsessive frequency with which they recur in her work. One is the movement outward, the journey; the other, its obverse, might be termed a movement inward, whereby an alien figure invades the initial context. Opposed as structures of action, both of these movements create for O'Connor's protagonists unprecedented situations, sudden crises which at their end often unveil the same image: the mocking face of the unsuspected double.

The strange and unknown intruders who turn up on the doorsteps of O'Connor's more respectable characters—beyond Bible salesmen and moronic nymphomaniacs, they may range from juvenile delinquents to stray bulls, from clubfooted fundamentalists to European refugees—are matched by the dark figures encountered at the climaxes of journeys, whether escaped convicts, angry black mothers, insane murderers, or statues of little Negroes. They make up a diverse group, certainly, extending from the apparently saintly to the clearly demonic, from the uncomprehending to the shrewdly knowing, from the masked confidence man to the blatantly leering mocker, from animal through human artifact. Yet different as their functions may be in individual stories, they possess in common an energy, a force: they become the galvanic centers of the works they inhabit, and in contrast to the more conventional protagonists they confront, they radiate an almost anarchic power. All are in some sense foreign, for they seem to embody a kind of knowledge the protagonists have lost touch with, and the most compelling are etched with the numinous, as if they are in contact with a mysterious country the more rational and "civilized" have never visited. They seem to demand recognition from the bemused intellectuals and genteel matrons they face: "Know me," they appear to threaten, "or be destroyed", or, even more terrifying, "Know me *and* be destroyed."

Now of course that country is a familiar one in O'Connor's fiction, and since these alien figures often come bearing a clear burden of religiosity, we might conclude quickly that her distinctive contribution to the modern tradition of the double is to give the motif a weight that is theological rather than psychological or simply moral. Yet her art is not, I think, so univalent. As "The Comforts of Home" alone shows, introducing the theological does not demand expelling the psychological. Quite the reverse: the revelations in O'Connor's works, so often precipitated by those double figures, come only when the consciousness of the protagonist, with all its presuppositions and defenses, is finally overthrown and a deeper awareness forces its way through. O'Connor clearly saw the human unconscious not only as, say, the repository of repressed sexual and aggressive urges, but as a realm of inherent theological dimension from which could come intimations of the demonic and the divine. Those potent doubles thus embody the link between the unknown within the self and the unknown beyond it, between the "other" hidden inside and that Other dimension which transcends the self, between the deepest roots of one's being and the furthest reaches of Being. As doppelgängers they thereby themselves acquire a double reference, pointing at once to the denials of the opposite numbers they face and to an unsuspected world beyond.

For this reason, O'Connor's more extreme characters tend to a curious family likeness whatever their precise theological weight. Criminals all, the ungovernable Sarah Ham, the murderous Misfit, and the old prophet Mason Tarwater, different as their functions may be, resemble one another far more closely than they do those apostles of moderation—Thomas, the grandmother, and the schoolteacher Rayber—that each of them confronts. And many readers have had trouble deciding whether Rufus Johnson of "The Lame Shall Enter First" is a demonic avenger or a prophetic savior. What this uncertainty suggests is that such distinctions are not in fact primary, that as imaginative figures O'Connor's doubles all spring from the same region of her creative mind and emerge with a Dionysian force that is anterior to whatever theological role they are asked to play. Invested with a mysterious power, their immediate and unvarying function is to intrude the perilous unknown into the bland surfaces of ordinary life.

It is as outsiders, radically antisocial and dangerous, often literally outlaws, that these dark figures proclaim their links with the tradition of the doppelgänger and make it hardly surprising that O'Connor acknowledged (however slightingly) Poe and (more warmly) Conrad and James among her literary forebears. The tradition has been persistent enough in the fiction of the past two centuries to establish some familiar contours, and seen in that larger context one telling characteristic of O'Connor's use of the motif leaps into sharp focus. What typically occurs in the relationship between the protagonist and his double is some form of intimate interaction, an increasing closeness, however hazardous or undesired, an expanding involvement that constitutes at least a tacit recognition of the claims of the second self. The captain of Conrad's "The Secret Sharer" can hardly bear to surrender his double, Leggatt, even though both his command of the ship and his sanity are threatened by the presence of the other; Spencer Brydon of James's "The Jolly Corner" feels a strong and growing interaction with his ghostly alter ego long before he encounters him face to face; the terrible Hyde waxes apace in the Dr. Jekyll of Stevenson's famous parable; and even the narrator of Poe's "William Wilson," for all his furious attempts to deny his meddling double, can never fully expunge either his feelings of affinity with the other Wilson or the memory of recognizing his own features on that foreign face. But one never finds this process in Flannery O'Connor. Possessing, as we have seen, much self-assurance but little real self-awareness, her protagonists meet the challenge of the double only with repudiation, outraged resistance, an increased hardening of attitude that presses the tensions of her stories to the bursting point. There is no gradual awakening, no glimmer or growth of recognition, only the sudden, shocking revelation as the veil is ripped aside.

Indeed, the characteristic action in O'Connor's fiction is the reverse of a process of confrontation between protagonist and "other": it is a progressive stiffening into "the extreme situation" (*Mystery and Manners*), the movement toward polar positions. The upshot of this is that her protagonists never truly reach either of the classic conclusions of the double tale: a final disintegration of personality (madness, suicide), or the reintegration and strengthening of the self. Images suggesting the reconciliation of self and other that do appear are highly ironic, as in that final paragraph of "The Comforts of Home" or in the analogous ending of "Greenleaf" where Mrs. May and the bull lie in a deadly embrace. Again, it is "The Artificial Nigger" that seems to provide the exception, a genuine reconciliation, but on closer examination the story turns out to confirm the rule. Mr. Head is indeed driven to an acceptance of the guilty self he has refused to know, the projection of "nigger" that the little statue both embodies and transforms, but rather than being integrated into his conscious identity, into all that is implied by *Head*, the new sense of self simply replaces the old. The "action of mercy" released by the statue both reveals to the old man his true identity as "a great sinner" and "cover[s] his pride like a flame and consume[s] it." In glimpsing both the divine love that comes from beyond the self and his own "true depravity," Mr. Head emerges from the story grasping the poles of a saving vision that has revealed to him his own incompleteness.

Yet O'Connor's stories rarely go this far. Much more typical are the two patterns noted earlier: a fatal refusal to recognize the double figure—pure Fortune destroys pure Pitts and dooms himself, Thomas denies Sarah Ham and shoots his mother—or conversely, a recognition that cannot finally be avoided, yet which leaves the protagonist adrift among the shattered bits of his inadequate self-definition—Joy Hopewell stripped of her symbolic leg, Sheppard of "The

Lame Shall Enter First" bereft of both his son and his secular liberalism. One comes to feel finally that the two sides of the self are so deeply inimical that no prolonged confrontation is possible, that O'Connor could hardly imagine a full reconciliation, that the fierce clash renewed in story after story had no permanent resolution this side of the grave. Psychologically, at least, Flannery O'Connor seems to have been an inveterate "Manichean."

Now it might be objected that the endings of those latter stories, for example, do open just such a possibility of reconciliation, that Joy Hopewell or Sheppard, freed of illusion through their encounters with the dark double, are at last capable of achieving a deeper, more genuinely integrated self. The strong sense of closure in these stories would not seem to invite speculation beyond their endings—although once begun, of course, anyone can play: isn't despair as likely a sequel as the more optimistic one outlined above? But whatever might be supposed to take place after a story's conclusion, it is obviously not *that* action that engaged O'Connor's imagination. Her stories and novels characteristically do not close on images of harmony and reconciliation, all passion spent, but in pain and violence and a profound sense of displacement, of permanent exile from the known and familiar, including the final displacement of death. And it is the surfacing of this memento mori at the end of all her works, whether literally on the page before us or metaphorically in those annihilations of identity, that provides a final clue to her singular use of the doppelgänger motif.

The protagonists of O'Connor's stories all cling to a narrow sense of order, whether the balanced social order of her many matrons or the dessicated rationalism of the intellectuals, for it allows them to feel safe from the terrors that they sense hover menacingly both within and without. The greatest of these terrors (for it ultimately includes all the others) is death, the chaos that swallows all human order along with the self that espouses it, that insists on the physical and finite nature of earthly existence. Here is the supreme triumph of the hylic, the final encompassing of the self by the world of matter. Much more comforting to deny death by projecting oneself into a perpetual future like Mr. Fortune, or by creating a new and beautifully unique self like Hulga Hopewell, or by retreating behind one's mother to develop a mastery over history like Thomas. If these are all attempts to transcend the common human fate, to achieve immortality, they are thereby also acts of hubris in which the mortal self usurps the powers of God. Thus the double figure is always a profound threat to the protagonist, for by definition he embodies all that has been denied in order to create the inflated invulnerable self. And thus, too, for Flannery O'Connor there can be no final reconciliation between them, for the impulse to rebel against death, to assert the self in the face of annihilation, to insist on the power of one's uniqueness can never be harmonized with the demand to submit, to risk the chaos of the physical, the dissolution of the self, and the certainty of death.

The "theological" sense of the doppelgänger motif is therefore much broader than the question of whether individual figures can be labeled divine or demonic. The double in O'Connor's fiction represents an ineluctable human dualism, the divided self that is the inheritance of fallen man, who is thereby doomed not only to incompleteness but to rending conflict. It is little comfort that those doubles often carry about them the overtones of the numinous, for their advent brings only the harrowing violence which ends not in a coming together but in a splitting apart, the sundering of the protagonist from his sense of himself and his world and even from life itself. O'Connor repeatedly stressed her concern as a writer with the operations of supernatural grace, but its workings, she said, are not those of "a healing property," not "warm and binding," but deeply "disruptive," "dark and divisive." The Christological passage she most often cited (Matt. 10:34) gives a precise description of the effect of her double figures: "Think not that I am come to send peace on earth: I came not to send peace, but a sword."

In a world of incomplete selves, we are thus led back to the grotesque not as a didactic metaphor of evil or Godlessness or false belief but as "an accurate description of the human condition, even at its best." That conclusion is implicit everywhere in O'Connor's work, but it surfaces clearly in her play with a traditional image of human wholeness. From Plato through the Renaissance to modern psychologists and poets, the image of the hermaphrodite has represented an ideal of human completeness, a reconciliation of the divisions within the self and between self and world. As Ernest Becker has put it, "It is a desire for a healing of the ruptures of existence, the dualism of self and body, self and other, self and world." The recurrent myth of the androgyne places that condition in an unfallen Golden Age or, sometimes using Gal. 3:28 ("There is neither male nor female: for ye are all one in Christ Jesus") in a mystical or future state. But when this androgynous ideal is incarnated in our actual fallen world, as it is in "A Temple of the Holy Ghost," it can only appear as, quite literally, a freak. O'Connor's use of the image in this story thus cuts in two directions at once: it is both a characteristically extreme metaphor for the suffering and limitation inherent in an inescapably physical existence (part of which paradoxically is our own *single* sexuality) and, simultaneously, an evocation of the state in which hermaphrodism is not grotesque but ideal, a contrast extended symbolically in the story through juxtaposed images of the suffering and the resurrected Christ. But in "A Temple of the Holy Ghost," as everywhere in O'Connor, we are condemned to live in this world, and to live as divided and incomplete selves. The freak serves as a kind of limited double for the twelve-year-old prepubescent protagonist who would like to believe that she exists as a disembodied mind, but if he introduces her to the religious dimension of even the most grotesque body (as suggested in the Pauline title), he cannot of course make her one with it. There is no final reconciliation between self and other in this world: one of the protagonist's last perceptions, typical of her detached and "mean" intelligence, is a dry notation of the piglike obesity of another character.

If for O'Connor this inner duality cannot finally be healed, there remains another possible way of at-onement: a denial so complete that it becomes an extirpation of one side of the self. Mr. Fortune's murder of his granddaughter in "A View of the Woods" expresses one form of this, the violent (and self-defeating) repudiation of the dark Pitts of the self. But the double figure may also embody the assertive consciousness, and when it does so its destruction is hardly less terrifying. This latter action is revealed most clearly not in the stories but in *The Violent Bear It Away*, a novel populated almost entirely by divided characters and doppelgängers. The rending struggle within young Tarwater which is the burden of the book is resolved not in an act of reintegration but in a ritual exorcism, a self-purification by fire that consumes the grinning "friend" who has shadowed him from the start. That friend is of course overtly presented as demonic, but he also embodies the rational, skeptical, rebellious, ironic side of Tarwater, and his destruction is a violent repudiation of an essential part of the boy. Tarwater achieves at the end a singleness of self and purpose, but the cost of that achievement is appalling.

It is a cost that Flannery O'Connor as a writer could not have afforded to pay. In her copy of Emmanuel Mounier's *The Character of Man*, she marked approvingly this passage: "When we say that thought is dialogue, we mean this quite strictly. We never think alone. The unspoken thought is a dialogue with someone who questions, contradicts, or spurs one on. This inner debate," Mounier continues, "may last a lifetime." Surely the radical tensions in O'Connor's fiction—its polar images, its extremities of conflict, its apocalyptic tendencies, its deeply self-divided heroes, and, not least, its numerous double figures—emerge from just such a creative inner dialogue, a dialogue that indeed seems to have lasted a lifetime. And if her fiction almost never presents images of self-integration, it is surely because, unlike young Tarwater, she could not still that ironic voice that questions and contradicts, that mocks and rebels and says no. "Does one's integrity ever lie in what he is not able to do?" she once asked rhetorically, and she responded, "I think that usually it does, for free will does not mean one will, but many wills conflicting in one man" (*Mystery and Manners*). O'Connor's own integrity as a writer lay in her projecting those conflicts into her fiction, dramatizing and exploring the clash without pretending to a spurious reconciliation she could not feel. One result is the obsessive recurrence of the double motif, but that creative inner tension finds even broader expression in some of the larger strategies of her fiction.

JEFFERSON HUMPHRIES

Proust, Flannery O'Connor, and the Aesthetic of Violence

Until the sun slipped finally below the tree line, Mrs. Turpin remained there with her gaze bent to them as if she were absorbing some abysmal life-giving knowledge. At last she lifted her head. There was only a purple streak in the sky. . . . A visionary light settled in her eyes. She saw the streak as a vast swinging bridge extending upward from the earth through a field of living fire. Upon it a vast horde of souls were rumbling toward heaven. There were whole companies of white-trash, clean for the first time in their lives, and bands of black niggers in white robes, and battalions of freaks and lunatics shouting and clapping and leaping like frogs. . . . She could see by their shocked and altered faces that even their virtues were being burned away. . . . At length she got down and turned off the faucet and made her slow way on the darkening path to the house. In the woods around her the invisible cricket choruses had struck up, but what she heard were the voices of the souls climbing upward into the starry field and shouting hallelujah.
—FLANNERY O'CONNOR, "Revelation"

O'CONNOR, PROUST, GRACE, AND THE DEVIL

If Proust is not, as I maintained at the outset of this study, a practitioner of the "mimetic" principle or principles—i.e., does not concern himself much with simulating "objective" realities or observe unities of time, place, or even character—Flannery O'Connor could be taken as an exemplary case of the writer who observes those principles scrupulously. Her fictions are so palpably anchored in a particular time and place as to color her readers' perceptions of the place itself. If

From *The Otherness Within: Gnostic Readings in Marcel Proust, Flannery O'Connor, and François Villon.* © 1983 by Louisiana State University Press.

111

her stories and novels appear fantastic to some, it is probably because they are unfamiliar with the rural South of which she wrote.

Despite this technical difference between Proust and O'Connor, not to mention breaches of culture and language, I have always had the feeling that there existed a profound kinship between them. Close examination reveals this as more than their common attraction for me. O'Connor shares Proust's belief in a spirit occulted in the flesh, though it might be argued that she states her case for it less arcanely. Though she insisted that her vision of humanity was not "Manichean" (her catchword for all things gnostic, which as a devout Catholic she regarded as heretical), she is interested above all in the distances which humans are at pains to place between themselves and the spiritual in themselves, the sacred in and around them, and in the terrible violence with which the Holy finally and inevitably erupts into their willfully profane lives. "The theologian," she wrote, "is interested specifically in the modern novel because there he sees reflected the man of our time, the unbeliever, who is nevertheless grappling in a desperate and usually honest way with intense problems of spirit." [*Mystery and Manners;* all further references to this text will be abbreviated as *MM.*] It is just this sort of ontological violence which overtakes Marcel. What Proust represents psychically, O'Connor represents physically, but Marcel's anxiety before Albertine and his lengthy analyses of it are closely related to the Misfit's homely theosophic peroration in "A Good Man Is Hard to Find," which culminates in murder, or the grandmother's discovery of Christian virtue in herself in the same story.

Of course, Proust does not share any of O'Connor's Catholic orthodoxy — or pretensions to it. Yet it is precisely in making those pretensions that she is closest to Proust, in the practice of her art and in spirit.

> I am always having it pointed out to me that life in Georgia is not at all the way I picture it, that escaped criminals do not roam the roads exterminating families, nor Bible salesmen prowl about looking for girls with wooden legs. . . . If the writer believes that our life is and will remain essentially mysterious, if he looks upon us as beings existing in a created order to whose laws we freely respond, then what he sees on the surface will be of interest to him only as he can go through it into an experience of mystery itself. His kind of fiction will always be pushing its own limits outward toward the limits of mystery, because for this kind of writer, the meaning of a story does not begin except at a depth where adequate motivation and adequate psychology and the various determinations have been exhausted. Such a writer will be interested in what we don't understand rather

than in what we do. . . . The kind of writer I am describimg will
use the concrete in a more drastic way. His way will much more obviously be the way of distortion.

[*MM*]

It is the writer's work to exhaust the concrete, to so wear out and stretch the
mimetic principle that the reader is forced to confront the inexplicable which
lies beyond, within, wherever one chooses to locate the place of *otherness,* of
gnostic realities.

This artistic principle of distortion, aesthetic violence, has something in
common with Maurice Blanchot's idea of communication. It entails a sense of
disintegration, dissolution, epistemological conflagration. For Blanchot, of
course, *la communication* is not an aesthetic principle and has nothing to do
with the content of a work of fiction but describes that strange and distinctly
gnostic (negative, antithetical) space which the act of reading conjures, delin-
eates as a negative, unknowable, indescribable, unentity — it is language betray-
ing its antithesis.

> The communication of the work is not in the fact of its becoming
> communicable, by reading, to a reader. The work is itself communi-
> cation, an intimacy in the struggle between the limits of the work as
> it is accessible and the excess of the work as it tends toward impossi-
> bility, between the form in which it is seized and the boundlessness
> in which it refuses itself, between the decision which is the being of
> beginning and the indecision which is the being of beginning again.
> This *violence* lasts as long as the work is a work, ever implacable, but
> also the calm of a harmony, strife which is the movement of under-
> standing, understanding which perishes as soon as it ceases to be the
> approach to that which cannot be understood [emphasis mine].

But O'Connor is not content to consider this as a purely secular phenomenon, or
as a simply literary one either.

She might find even more to agree with in Georges Bataille's idea of writing
as transgression, an incendiary act against the logos of positivism and the means
by which men may transcend words and themselves in the contemplation of an
absence. Bataille is careful to differentiate this "Absence" from "nothingness."
Violence is the only way of attaining the transcendental contact with it which
Bataille calls "sovereignty." Where physical violence, murder, is proscribed, literary violence must take its place. "Literature (fiction)," writes Bataille, "has replaced what used to be the life of the spirit, while poetry (the disorder of words)

has replaced the state of actual trance." "My tension resembles, in a sense, a mad desire to laugh, it differs little from the passions with which the heroes of Sade burn, and yet it is very near the passions of martyrs or saints."

I evoke Blanchot and Bataille not to argue that O'Connor or Proust ever read or would have read or approved of them. O'Connor would probably have been horrified to find herself quoted in the same paragraph with them, as she was at John Hawkes's statement that "her muse is the Devil." Still, though she was bound to deny the letter of his thesis, she was willing to admit that Hawkes's intuition in stating it was correct. Her kinship with Hawkes, with Bataille, with Blanchot, with Proust, and with the mythic Satan as well lies in the idea of transgression, literature as a hostile, aggressive gesture towards an overweening and distortedly positivistic status quo. Positivism is just as despotic and corrosive for O'Connor as for Bataille. Where Bataille would assimilate the church to that positivism, O'Connor does just the opposite. She sees the modern church as forced to adopt a stance of violent dissidence; the truths of the spirit are mines, time bombs occulted in all the most apparently safe and unspiritual places and persons—many an O'Connor character turns out to be an unwitting guerilla, sacrificing him or herself for a spirit and a spiritual truth repeatedly and assiduously denied.

Indeed, O'Connor was more than willing to concur with Hawkes that the devil, patron spirit of violence and destruction, occupied a major, perhaps the major role in her fiction. She was also careful to point out that evil cannot but serve good by forcing man to apprehend his own spirit, catalyzing that corrosive demesmerizement which she calls grace. Bataille would doubtless prefer to describe it as the contemplation of an absence. But there is nothing implicitly incompatible about the terminologies—provided one does not happen to be a dogmatic Catholic. John Hawkes has made a similar point:

> Since I have mentioned that Flannery O'Connor does not agree with my notion of her central fictional allegiance, it is only right to say that our disagreement may not be so extensive after all, and that she has written that, "Those moments (involving awareness of the Holy) are prepared for—by me anyway—by the intensity of evil circumstances." She also writes, "I suppose the devil teaches most of the lessons that lead to self-knowledge." And further that "her" devil is the one who goes about "piercing pretensions, not the devil who goes about seeking whom he may devour." If Flannery O'Connor were asked where she would locate the center of her creative impulse, she might reply "in the indication of Grace." But then again she might not. And I suspect that she would not reply at all to such a

question. It may be, too, that I have been giving undue stress to the darker side of her imaginative constructions, and that the devil I have been speaking of is only a metaphor, a way of referring to a temperament strong enough and sympathetic enough to sustain the work of piercing pretension.

"Piercing pretension," "Grace," "devil," are finally all weak and insufficient figurative names for something much less prosaic and domesticable than a "temperament," literary or criminal, something too horrifically and unnervingly negative, unnameable, for even as hardy a soul as Hawkes to contemplate. For John Hawkes finally takes refuge in the very positivism his fiction confounds, in reducing the devil to a metaphor—rather than considering that the Evil One might represent an effort to name, and so domesticate, through mythical narrative, that which defies nomination. If Flannery O'Connor would remain silent rather than "locate the center of her creative impulse," as I with Hawkes believe she would have, it is because, a stronger writer than Hawkes, she knew the question's answer could not be said.

THE GROTESQUENESS OF UNBELIEF, OR, THE SACRED AS A NEGATION OF A NEGATION

O'Connor sees "the man of our time" as having created the dualistic world which he occupies in her stories. His darkness, ignorance, distance from the Holy are consequences of his own unbelief. His spiritual velleity and intellectual agnosticism put modern man in the very state of grotesque decrepitude in which gnostic theology would place him. The natural world is good because it emanates from God. This is a Catholic, not a gnostic sentiment. Evil, however, in O'Connor's universe, has made the natural world and the human beings in it grotesque; it has distorted and occluded their goodness. Evil can only come into being as a negation of the world, the Holy. It is derivative and can only deny, vitiate. It can only become intelligible as a destructive force and a necessary consequence of our moral freedom [MM]. Evil is what blinds us to the Holy and it is the state of blindness. But we have blinded ourselves. For O'Connor, man has been his own demiurge, the author of his own fall, the keeper of his own cell. Which is not to say that evil has no physical reality. It is just as physically real as good. Believing a thing, choosing freely to believe it, does indeed make it so. Choices freely made, convictions freely held, are for O'Connor moral acts with ferociously physical, as well as spiritual, consequences.

Her fictions can be read as a catalog of the unbeliever in his many incarnations. In addition to the simple atheist, there is the one "who recognizes a divine

being not himself, but who does not believe that this being can be known ana-
gogically or defined dogmatically or received sacramentally. Spirit and matter
are separated for him [*MM*]." Again, she sees this type as a self-made gnostic.
Finally, there is the sort which holds the greatest interest for her, the "modern
man who can neither believe nor contain himself in unbelief and who searches
desperately, feeling about in all experience for the lost God [*MM*]." This is the
archetype of the gnostic, a seeker after a knowledge that cannot be known.

The chief consequence of this partly willful, partly inherited alienation
from the sacred is that the sacred can only intrude upon human perception as a
violence, a rending of the fabric of daily life, a negation of the negation which is
evil (albeit a passive, quiescent evil). It bruises both the spirit and the body
which have based themselves in unbelief.

For Proust, it is time and space which have made monsters of men, made
them grotesque. "At least, if enough force was left me to accomplish my work, I
would not fail firstly to describe men (even were it necessary to make them
resemble monstrous beings) as occupying such a considerable place, next to the
very restricted one reserved for them in space, a place on the contrary prolonged
beyond measure — since they touch, simultaneously, like giants immersed in the
years, epochs so distant, between which so many many days have intervened — in
Time." O'Connor says much the same thing, that she has no choice but to describe men as freaks because they live in a world bereft of belief — "which doubts
both fact and value," so that "instead of reflecting a balance from the world
around him, the novelist now has to achieve one from felt balance inside *himself*" [*MM*]. The novelist cannot but see a distorted world, cannot but see men
as monsters, the more so as he feels himself to be in monstrous discord with that
world.

> The problem for such a novelist will be to know how far he can dis-
> tort without destroying, and in order not to destroy, he will have to
> descend far enough into himself to reach those underground springs
> that give life to his work. This *descent into himself* will, at the same
> time, be a descent into his region. It will be *a descent through the
> darkness of the familiar into a world where, like the blind man cured
> in the gospels, he sees men as if they were trees, but walking.* This is
> the beginning of vision, and I feel it is a vision which we in the South
> must at least try to understand if we want to participate in the con-
> tinuance of a vital Southern literature. I hate to think that in twenty
> years Southern writers too may be writing about men in gray-flannel
> suits and may have lost their ability to see that these gentlemen are

even greater freaks than what we are writing about now. I hate to think of the day when the Southern writer will satisfy the tired reader [emphasis mine].

[*MM*]

The work of the novelist is not meant, or ought not to be meant to soothe or satisfy but to upset and perturb. The writer's vision is a violence wreaked on the world, the violence of perception, the brutality of the sacred bursting into the lives and senses of self-anesthetized men and giving them visions which reveal the world and the people in it as strange players in a hugely terrible mystery.

THE "TAINT" OF VISION: THE ARTIST AS CRIMINAL AND LEPER

The impact of that apprehension of the ineffable ravages the writer more than his characters, for it isolates him, estranges him, deforms him in the eyes of the world. It infects him like love, which Proust called an agony to be cultivated to the point at which disease and sufferer are indistinguishable. The writer and the lover (for Proust) and the seer, the believer (for O'Connor) are untouchables, a "citizen of an unknown country," as Proust describes the composer Vinteuil, inhabiting "a closed realm, with impenetrable borders," as he said of the painter Elstir. The business of all these visionaries is to wreak havoc on their own perceptions, and the perceptions of others. In both ways they rend the world, as the conduit through which the Holy enters and transforms it. This—their art—is a curative, redemptive gesture. It may not appear so, but this is because the advanced state of the malady makes it impossible to treat the patient without maiming him.

The para-Freudian interpretation of Proust's artistic stance which I tried to make in the last chapter would seem to hold true for O'Connor as well, notwithstanding her protestations of Christian orthodoxy. If her work does not structurally resemble Proust's in almost any way—it is rather linear than circular; it can by no stretch of the imagination be read as autobiographical, though it must inevitably be involved in a specular relation with the subject who made it as it is with the subject who reads it—her work reflects a fascination with sickness, with disabilities of mind, spirit, and matter. Both Proust and O'Connor were invalids for most of their adult lives. This is bound to have something to do with their sense of the sacred as physically destructive.

The "lines" traced by O'Connor's narratives end so often in death that she has been criticized for resorting too frequently and facilely to destruction of her characters as a way of ending her stories. This sort of criticism ignores the internal necessity of death, the intense desire for it in so many of her characters. Death, or maiming, a step in the direction of death, is askesis, a movement towards the Holy. In her stories, her world, death is the force which invades and undoes the negation of unbelief. Death appears as a negative force only because we see it from an already negatively defined context, which is our own unbelief. The unbeliever—which describes most of her critics—reads O'Connor's stories much as the atheist Mr. Paradise watches the boy Bevel drown himself in "The River." Paradise's unbelief is emblemized in the cancer over his ear which he pointedly displays before the faithful to mock the alleged healing powers of their minister; his name casts a grim irony over his own positivistic attitudes, throwing the corruption of his physical body into relief. He tries to rescue Harry / Bevel from "the rich red river of Jesus' Blood," the river "that was made to carry sin," "a River full of pain itself, pain itself." But the boy—who in baptism has taken the name of the preacher who baptized him—has discovered in his immersion a calling, "the calling": "to Baptize himself and to keep on going this time until he found the kingdom of Christ in the river." This discovery, from Mr. Paradise's vantage point, looks like death. But Bevel in fact leaves Mr. Paradise behind "like some ancient water-monster"; leaves him in place and spirit.

The criminals of Miss O'Connor's world, monsters remarkable in their reality, doers of violence not to themselves directly but to the unbelieving world which offers no other issue to the striving of their spirits, destroy and torment for the pleasure of spite, which is no pleasure at all ("Shut up Bobby Lee, it's no real pleasure in life"). They destroy in desperation and rage at their own unbelief. Unwittingly, though, as ministers of violence they are instruments of good. So, ironically, does the Devil undo his own designs. The Misfit, or the Bible salesman of "Good Country People," brings about a spiritual askesis in the people whose lives he invades and upsets. The force of his intrusion ferrets individuals out of their elaborately articulated despair and philistinism, out of the pettiness in which they have sought refuge from the horrible burden of believing, communicating with the Holy. Bringing death, the Misfit brings the grandmother of "A Good Man Is Hard to Find" to a searing intuition of the sacred, out of the old-womanly selfishness which has defined her character throughout the story. " 'Jesus!' the old lady cried. 'You've got good blood! I know you wouldn't shoot a lady! I know you come from nice people! Pray! Jesus, you ought not to shoot a lady. I'll give you all the money I've got.' " She reaches such a clarity of vision that she is able to recognize what she and the Misfit have in common, and to pity his hopelessness: "the grandmother's head cleared for an instant. . . . She murmured, 'Why you're one of my own babies. You're one of my own children.' " For the instant before she dies, the sacred takes hold of this old lady and for perhaps the first time in her life she is filled with charity. The Misfit has been the instrument of her salvation, and not entirely unwittingly. He says that "she would of been a good woman if it had of been somebody there to shoot her every minute of her life." He knows that he is sending the old woman off to heaven. This is why he finds no pleasure in killing and destruction. He knows that evil can have no positive impact, cannot redound to its own benefit. If it has any impact, it is as the unwitting servant of the good it despises — and secretly longs for. Evil, for O'Connor as for Milton, is comical. All its violent antics are, in the long view, so much futile slapstick. It cannot affect the ultimate outcome of things. But evil for O'Connor bears a greater dignity than mere unbelief, because there is some force of will and spirit behind it, and deliberate choice — and because genuine evil knows perfectly well that it cannot but serve the good. The preacher of "The River" admonishes his audience to "believe Jesus or the Devil . . . Testify to one or the other!"

Those who choose Jesus and deliberately minister to others who would choose him are hardly more benign than the Misfit himself. The Reverend Bevel Summers cautions his congregations in "The River" that "you can't leave your pain in the river." "The River of Life, made out of Jesus' Blood" is "a River full of pain itself." To be saved, one must enter that river and be part of it. Only the river of pain and trouble and blood moves towards the Kingdom of Christ. " 'If it's this River of Life you want to lay your pain in, then come up,' the preacher said, 'and lay your sorrow here. But don't be thinking this is the last of it because this old red river don't end here. This old red suffering stream goes on, you people, slow to the Kingdom of Christ. This old red river is good to Baptize in, good to lay your faith in, good to lay your pain in, but it ain't this muddy water here that saves you.' " "You won't be the same again," he warns the boy Harry, whom he is about to baptize Bevel "in the river of suffering." Nor — such at least must have been her hope — nor will the reader who deeply feels O'Connor's fiction be the same after reading it. It might seem at first a joke, as the river seems to Harry-Bevel. But it is no joke. Her story means, like the river, to make us "count," even if it does so by forcing us to "swallow some dirt," to feel what it's like to "tread on nothing," to suffer literarily the experience of death by drowning.

> He stopped and thought suddenly: it's another joke, it's another joke! He thought how far he had come for nothing and he began to hit and splash and kick the filthy river. His feet were already treading on nothing. He gave one low cry of pain and indignation. Then he heard a shout and turned his head and saw something like a giant pig bounding after him, shaking a red and white club and shouting. He plunged under once and this time, the waiting current caught him like a long gentle hand and pulled him forward and

down. For an instant he was overcome with surprise; then since he was moving quickly and knew that he was getting somewhere, all his fury and fear left him.

The monstrous figure of Mr. Paradise ("like a giant pig") strikes a discordantly comical note in this hauntingly severe vignette. It is not Bevel-Harry's death which is comic, but Mr. Paradise's failure to understand its significance.

EPIPHANIES AND THE UNDERWORLD

The fury and fearsomeness of O'Connor's work is meant to submerge us in an epiphany more consciously religious than Proust's but just as firmly based on an aesthetic principle of madness, violence, and what James Hillman [in *The Dream and the Underworld*] calls a fall into the underworld, the world of death, dreams, and the Holy. Hillman finds it useful to speak of our active, wakeful selves as Herculean, and of the persona in which we dream and otherwise enter the deathworld as Orphean. Hercules puts aside all action to enter the kingdom of death—as Orpheus, he must submit to death's authority to gain entry. Proust had his own, remarkably similar language for these faces of the personality:

> The being who was reborn in me when, with such a shudder of happiness, I heard that noise common to both the spoon touching the dish and the hammer striking the wheel, to the unevenness of step of the flagstones in the Guermantes courtyard and of the baptistery of Saint Mark's, etc., that being is nourished only by the essences of things, in them only does it find its sustenance, its delight. It languishes in the observation of the present where the senses cannot bring it this essence, in the consideration of a past which the intelligence dries up, in the anticipation of a future which the will constructs out of fragments of the present and past from which it has withdrawn still more of their reality, retaining of them only that which serves the utilitarian and narrowly human end which it assigns them. But if a noise, an odor, heard or smelled before, should happen to be heard or smelled again, at once in the present and the past, real without being contemporaneous, ideal without being abstract, then the permanent and habitually hidden essence of things is liberated, and our true self which, sometimes for very long, had seemed dead but was not entirely, awakens, stirs itself, receiving the celestial nourishment which is brought to it. One minute free from the order of time has re-created in us, by the perception of it, the man liberated from the order of time. And we understand this man's

confidence in his joy, even if the mere taste of a madeleine cake does not logically appear to contain the reasons for that joy, we understand that the word "dead" has no meaning for him; situated outside of time, what can he fear from the future?

This *être de mort* can only be nourished by concealed essences, a comestible lode situated somewhere beyond the laws of time, outside the day-world—in the realm of Pluto, then, Hades. Hillman has some interesting things to say about the mythology and etymology of death and its god.

> Hades' name was rarely used. At times he was referred to as "the unseen one," more often as Pluto ("wealth," "riches") or as Trophonios ("nourishing"). These disguises of Hades have been taken by some interpreters to be covering euphemisms for the fear of death, but then why this particular euphemism and not some other? Perhaps Pluto is a description of Hades, much as Plato understood this God. Then, Pluto refers to the hidden wealth or the riches of the invisible. Hence, we can understand one reason why there was no cult and no sacrifice to him—Hades was the wealthy one, the giver of nourishment to the soul. Sometimes, he was fused with Thanatos ("Death") of whom Aeschylus wrote, "Death is the only God who loves not gifts and cares not for sacrifices or libation, who has no altars and receives no hymns . . . " (frg. *Niobe*). On vase paintings when Hades is shown, he may have his face averted, as if he were not even characterized by a specific physiognomy. All this "negative" evidence does coalesce to form a definite image of a void, an interiority or depth that is unknown but nameable, there and felt even if not seen. Hades is not an absence, but a hidden presence—even an invisible fullness.
>
> Etymological investigations into the root word for *death demon* show it to mean "hider." To grasp better the ways in which Hades hides invisibly in things, let us take apart this concept, listening for the hidden connections, the metaphors, within the word *hidden* itself: (1) buried, shrouded, concealed from eyesight, whether a corpse or a *mysterium;* (2) occult, esoteric, concealed in the sense of secret; (3) that which per se cannot be seen: non-visible as non-spatial, nonextended; (4) without light: dark, black; (5) that which cannot be seen on inspection, i.e., blocked, censored, forbidden, or obscured; (6) hidden, as contained within (interior) or as contained below (inferior), where the Latin *cella* ("subterranean storeroom") is cognate with the Old Irish *cuile* ("cellar") and *cel* ("death"), again cognate

with our *hell;* (7) that which is experienced with dread and terror, a void, a nothing; (8) that which is experienced as hiding, e.g., withdrawing, turning away from life; (9) stealth, surreptitiousness, deceit, such as the hidden motives and unseen connections of Hermes. In short, Hades, the hidden hider, presides over both the crypt and cryptic, which gives to Heraclitus' phrase (frg. 123): "Nature loves to hide" (*physis kryptesthai philei*), a subtle and multiple implication indeed.

Ancient myth and modern psychology agree that there is no time in the under-world. So it makes no sense to think of the underworld as the setting of the after-life. It is rather "the afterthoughts within life." "It is not a far-off place or judgment over our actions but provides that place of judging now, and within, the inhibiting reflection interior to our actions."

The underworld is contiguous and simultaneous with the day-world. Hades is a mirror image, a negative image of Zeus. Every event in the upper world is reflected in, has a reflection in the lower world, the difference between the two being a difference of perspective rather than of substance. The spiritual perspective is the one which is without time or light. The epiphanic moment, for Proust and for O'Connor, is that moment at which a sudden breach in the upper world occurs, dropping both reader and character—and writer, for that matter—into the occulted underworld, the moment at which the supernatural, the invisible, the spiritual, erupts into the consciousness of reader or writer or character, not necessarily taking hold but reminding us that it exists. O'Connor's stories frequently end with a literal sinking: Harry-Bevel's drowning in "The River" ("treading on nothing"), the grandmother collapsing in a ditch after the Misfit shoots her; or with a rejection of the world and its light such as Haze Motes' self-inflicted blindness. Sometimes the netherworld creeps rather than bursts into the picture, as at the end of "A Stroke of Good Fortune"—a fine story to which both O'Connor and her critics have been unkind, perhaps because it is more dramatically subtle and moves more slowly than her other fictions. The only movement in the story is that of a woman climbing a flight of stairs. Her painful ascent is accompanied by the gradual realization that she is pregnant, something which she has taken every precaution to avoid and which she has always dreaded fiercely.

She sat on the step, clutching the banister spoke while the breath came back into her a thimbleful at a time and the stairs stopped see-sawing. She opened her eyes and gazed down into the dark hold, down to the very bottom where she had started up so long ago. "Good Fortune," she said in a hollow voice that echoed along all the levels of the cavern, "Baby." "Good Fortune, Baby," the three echoes leered. Then she recognized the feeling again, a little roll. It was as if it were not in her stomach. It was as if it were out nowhere in nothing, out nowhere, resting and waiting, with plenty of time.

Hillman, in a brilliant and radical revision of Freudian theory, redefines Thanatos so that the pathology of this aesthetic which I tried to elaborate in the last chapter is rendered moot by being established as not at all pathological but perfectly normal. "Because his realm was conceived as the final end of each soul, Hades is the final cause, the purpose, the very *telos* of every soul and every soul process. If so, then *all* psychic events have a Hades aspect, and not merely the sadistic or destructive events that Freud attributed to Thanatos. All soul processes, everything in the psyche, moves towards Hades." Hillman has a point here, but one that would seem more apt in some cases than in others. Which is to say that I remain convinced that the gnostic aesthetic, absorbed as it is with what Hillman calls Hades, does represent a deviation from the norm—though I would be as hard pressed as anyone to say what that "norm" might be. Hillman himself admits that this reflective, oneiric mode of consciousness affects some individuals much more than it does others. For those whom it does affect, says Hillman, it is accompanied by a profound sense of loss—another observation which agrees entirely with my readings of Proust and O'Connor. "The movement from three-dimensional physical perception to the two dimensions of psychical reflection is first felt as a loss: *thymos* gone, we hunger, bewailing, paralyzed, repetitive. We want blood. Loss does characterize underworld experiences, from mourning to the dream, with its peculiar feeling of incompleteness, as if there is still more to come that we didn't get, always a concealment within it, a lost bit. A life that is lived in close connection with the psyche does indeed have an ongoing feeling of loss." Whether the sense of loss—which is also the sense of "the presence of the void"—is cause or effect of a "close connection with the psyche" is impossible to say.

What O'Connor shares with Proust is the use of the written word as a dark glass, to bring us into contact with our underworld selves, our "dead" selves. Literature and every literary activity, reading or writing, is innately reflective and introspective. As Proust said, "In reality, every reader is, when he reads, reading himself. The work of the writer is only a sort of optical instrument which he offers to the reader that the latter may discern that which, without the book, he might not have seen in himself." Proust and O'Connor use this innate property of literature to bring us into contact with a part of ourselves which many of us might prefer to ignore. Their fictions are elaborately constructed chutes through which we are supposed, if not to fall into the underworld, to gain some sense of its reality. It is entirely appropriate that the images by which we make that transition should be violent, even repugnant—what is being represented is "the collapse of the corporeal."

The reader's willingness to subject himself to unpleasant imagery, or simply to undertake the task of reading, must in some sense derive from the sense of loss which Hillman, O'Connor, and Proust have all pointed to as a crucial part of their work. We enter the realm of death to recover something as Orpheus entered it to bring back Eurydice. He failed to bring her into the day-world by forgetting to observe the rules set down by Pluto; he reverted to the rules of the upper world before he was in it, and so lost what he had gone to find. Absence, loss, lack, have substance only in the place of the dead. We can go there and "see" it, but we cannot bring it out. The sense of loss is far greater as we come out than it was before our descent. So it drives us back into the underworld. Surely O'Connor never conceived that her fictions would precipitate the kind of extreme and physical rejection of the world that Haze Motes experiences; it must be safe to say that she neither wanted nor expected readers to blind themselves with lye. More probably she wanted us to have some sense, like Ruby Hill, of staring down a black stairwell, hearing a voice at once ours and not ours, some part of us speaking from "the very bottom where she had started up so long ago," "out nowhere in nothing, out nowhere, resting and waiting, with plenty of time."

JOHN BURT

What You Can't Talk About

Chief among the temptations that Satan offers Jesus in Luke 4 is the opportunity to prove himself by signs to be the son of God. Setting him upon the pinnacle of the Temple in Jerusalem, Satan taunts, "If you are the Son of God, throw yourself down from here." What he requires is not simply that Jesus perform a stunt to demonstrate his more than human powers, for they both know that stunts of any sort would not suffice to decide the issue. What Satan requires is more rigorous: he demands that Jesus prove himself by fulfilling, on conditions laid down by Satan himself, the very prophecies Jesus claims to have come to fulfill, and he quotes Psalm 91 as an instance of what he expects.

Christ's response to the learned devil appears to evade the question. "You shall not tempt the Lord your God," he says, quoting Deut. 6, and leaving it undecided whether the "you" he speaks of is Satan or himself. What he means, of course, is that to demand that God prove himself is to commit the sin of Pride, for we cannot sit in judgment of God, and we cannot set conditions for him, even when we are only asking him to be as good as his word. There are, Jesus implicitly argues, no ways to demonstrate the validity of transcendental claims, and to look for such ways is to mistake the nature of the claims and to extend (whether through hubris or through a simple category mistake) the rules of argument and the conventions of language into areas where discourse of any sort is impossible. Jesus meets Satan's challenge by showing that the question which underlies it—the question of how we prove anything about God—is what Wittgenstein would have called a philosophical question, a question which no conceivable reply can suffice to answer, a question whose answer can be shown

Published for the first time in this volume. © 1986 by John Burt.

125

but not spoken. The beliefs for which Jesus stands cannot be phrased as propositions in any ordinary sense of the term, for they do not pick out any point in logical space but instead present the shape of that space as a whole.

One might argue from this passage that matters of faith differ in kind from matters of fact, that religious belief is not simply factual opinion or a weakened form of knowledge, but something entirely unlike knowledge and not capable of, and not requiring, demonstration or proof. Because we cannot subject God to rules, no remark can describe him, no argument can bear on him. For a God whom we judge with our reason is perhaps no less an idol than one we make with our hands. God is not an object of examination, and statements about God do not refer to God as statements of fact refer to states of affairs.

If such statements are not capable of characterizing God, they are nevertheless capable of characterizing the believer's faith; they are capable of showing how his world looks, even if they do not pick out any part of that world. Professions of faith commit the believer to his belief, and therefore indicate his moral state. Statements of fact, on the other hand, commit him only to the rules and methods of rationality, and say nothing else in particular about him. The former give access to the subject, the latter circumscribe objects, and we cannot subject one to the determination of the other. According to this line of thought, then, the believer believes not because he has grounds for doing so but because his belief is the ground and basis of his other knowledge. It is what makes his knowledge possible, and it is also what makes knowledge something he wants to have. He does not believe what he believes because the world is the way it is; rather, he believes what he believes because he is the way he is, and the nature of his world is a consequence, not a cause, of his belief.

Happy as Christ's answer might be for the believer, the unbeliever can take small comfort from it, for if belief is not subject to proof by any method of verification he may share with believers, then he is offered no avenue toward belief and no method of choosing between competing forms of belief. The unbeliever may recognize the difficulty of belief, but he cannot find any evidence capable of leading him to believe, and will find himself, so long as he relies on his own faculties, forever among those, as Christ says in Mark 4, to whom the Kingdom of Heaven is described only in parables, so that try as they might they will always see but not perceive, hear but not understand.

It is because the idea of belief is subject to this difficulty, because belief instantly takes us out of what Blake calls demonstration and into what he calls inspiration, that literary works by authors for whom belief is central tend to provoke controversy over that belief, especially when those works are, as Flannery O'Connor's are, specifically aimed at unbelieving readers. If demonstration, or for that matter, language, is not capable of doing justice to transcendence, then the only way that we critics can know that the author's claim is not delusory is by our inability to convince anybody that it is genuine. And this leaves us just where we least want to be. We stand up there, a little dizzy, on the pinnacle of the temple, reasoning with the devil, secretly afraid we might fall after all.

The difficulty of human contact with transcendence is, of course, Flannery O'Connor's central subject. It is what is at issue in *The Violent Bear It Away* between Tarwater and his mysterious friend (and, in an attenuated form, between Tarwater and Rayber), and it is also what is at issue in *Wise Blood* between Hazel Motes and himself. The same issue is debated hotly, and in similar terms, by O'Connor's critics. It is no surprise, then, that the struggle between Tarwater and his friend over the nature and value of religious belief can be translated into the struggle in the criticism over whether Flannery O'Connor's stories and novels can fairly be described as works governed by orthodox Christian habits of thought.

To claim contact with transcendence is to leap outside of the rules which govern the conventional discourse of unbelievers and to speak a language which from without must be indistinguishable from nonsense, even if it is coherent and precise from within. What I propose to do here is to examine whether any author—or any character not subjected to debilitating irony by the author—can make this leap without interrupting the application of those rules without which interpretation, or even appreciation, is impossible.

I

One of the stories O'Connor wrote for her master's thesis, "The Turkey" (then called "The Capture") demonstrates the uncertainties we have just introduced, not only posing them to the reader as an interpretive problem but also presenting them to the central character as the predicament his story embodies.

The protagonist, an innocent and rather silly child named Ruller McFarney, appears to us as the possessor of an active fancy formed by matinee westerns. Our first view of him shows him levelling his six-shooter at an imaginary rustler he has just lassoed about the ankles. Immediately a more worthy object of capture, a wounded turkey, presents itself. "If only I had a gun!" the child thinks, who had only a paragraph before been brandishing one. The point of this juxtaposition, of course, is to poke fun at his childish imagination, and the story continues to undercut his imagination not only for its inability to answer real desires (say, to capture the turkey) but also for its tendency to provoke theological errors.

Stalking the lame turkey as it moves through the bushes, Ruller imagines what his parents' reaction will be when he brings the bird home, and imagines his own nonchalant response. Up to this point, his fantasies simply fulfill his wishes; they present him not only as having surprised and pleased his parents with his capture but also as having vindicated himself in their eyes, as having proved to them that, in pointed contrast to his brother Hane, he would not turn out "bad."

Only when his wishes are thwarted do his imaginations take on a religious character. Having run into a tree and lost the bird, he gives himself up to sullen meditations:

> He kicked a stone away from his foot. He'd never see the turkey now.
> He wondered why he had seen it in the first place if he wasn't going
> to be able to get it. It was like somebody had played a dirty trick on
> him.

Gradually, after some childish profanity, and a scene in which Ruller imagines himself responding to his parents' ridicule by kicking somebody in the legs, he comes to conclusions about who has played this trick on him: "God could go around sticking things in your face and making you chase them all afternoon for nothing." He decides that God intended the turkey as a sign to him that he was indeed going "bad," and he sets about imagining ways to shock his pious relatives.

Looking around as if someone might be hiding in the bushes and hearing all of his blasphemy, Ruller discovers the turkey lying dead on the ground. All his earlier fantasies return, but he adds to them the belief that the recovery of the bird was a divinely ordained sign of his own election:

> Maybe it was to keep him from going bad. Maybe God wanted to
> keep him from that.
>
> Maybe God had knocked it out right there where he'd see it when
> he got up.
>
> Maybe God was in the bush now, waiting for him to make up his
> mind. Ruller blushed. He wondered if God could think he was a very
> unusual child. He must. He found himself suddenly blushing and
> grinning and he rubbed his hand over his face quick to make himself
> stop. If You want me to take it, he said, I'll be glad to.

Ruller imagines the various good works God must be planning for him—founding a school for boys who might be "going bad," giving money to beggars (one of whom, after a fashion, conveniently appears), and so on—but just as his fantasies lead him to the point where he feels as if the ground no longer needs to be under him, some country boys of the sort who might have been sent to his school steal his turkey from him. No longer someone who can lasso rustlers or catch turkeys, Ruller runs home, fearing capture himself, "certain that Something Awful was tearing behind him with its arms rigid and its fingers ready to clutch."

The moral of this extended joke on Ruller seems to be that imagination is folly. It is silly of Ruller to presume to set up the capture of the turkey as a test of what God intends for him. It would be easy to stop here and say either with Burns "This story implies that there is no God," or with May "This story implies that there is a God but he moves in mysterious ways." But if it is wrong for Ruller to project meanings onto natural events and to assume that catching the turkey shows how he stands with God, then it is also wrong for the author to project meaning onto those same events, to say that they prove either that God's ways are mysterious or that there is no God. For to say that the loss of the turkey proves that there are no divinely appointed meanings is no less to impose a meaning on the events than it would be to say that capturing the turkey is indeed a sign of divine favor. There is, after all, no way of designing a proof that there is no design; if there were, Ruller would be right to say that nature intends to teach him a lesson, but he would simply have learned the wrong one.

Even the purport of this lesson is hard to understand, for the two possible conclusions are hard to untangle from each other. No possible test can distinguish the proposition "There are no purposes in nature," from "There are purposes in nature, but they are always mysterious." We can no more say whether the intent of the story is "religious" or "ironic" than Ruller can say with certainty that the appearance of the turkey was (or was not) a divinely-sent sign to prevent him from "going bad."

The "Something Awful" that chases Ruller at the end is clearly just himself, but its exact status is difficult to define. As with the turkey, we can neither take it seriously nor refuse to do so. Certainly Ruller is a fool, and he runs from himself just as the turkey ran from him. But if God really *did* speak to us through signs, they could not be very different from this "Something Awful" (although they would probably be very different from the turkey). They would have to look like vanity or deviant psychology, and no clear test could prove them to be of divine origin. "Something Awful" is a sign of our inability to determine what it is we see. It is a powerful absence the imagination creates out of its failures, a shock carried into our hearts like that of Wordsworth's Boy of Winander feels when the owls no longer imitate his voice. It is not the nothing that is not there but, hilariously, the nothing that is.

What we have in this "Something Awful" is not a symbol which represents a transcendental thing but an indication that the limits of symbol-making power have been reached. It does not refer to anything outside of language but rather to the discomfort and uneasiness we suffer within language when we are stricken by hunger for a transcendental sanction. It is crucially important, however, that we distinguish between this half-hilarious and half-chilling suspension of the symbolic function and a simple eruption of nonsense. Wittgenstein distinguishes in the *Tractatus* between nonsensical propositions, which is to say propositions which are in trivial ways poorly formed, and propositions which have no sense because they attempt to address questions, such as the classic philosophical questions about the nature of the real, the true, or the beautiful, which cannot be formulated in language. Language can only present what it is capable of making crucial discriminations about and thus, although it is capable of describing states of affairs (which, since they are parts of logical space, are capable of being discriminated within logical space), it is not capable of making discriminations about matters at its own level of generality or higher, questions which, like the philosophical questions, concern the nature of logical space as a whole.

As this suspension of the symbol-making power does not produce the trivialest form of nonsense, so "faith" as O'Connor understands it is not merely the trivialest collapse of reason. It does not involve, she wrote to Alfred Corn on June 16, 1962, "any leap into the absurd," for O'Connor finds what she believes "reasonable to believe, even though these beliefs are beyond reason." What faith does involve sounds more like skepticism than like belief, for what she means by the term is freedom from confinement in the limitations of one's own ideas, no matter how true those ideas seem to be. Faith is the freedom to withhold one's final assent from the determinism of one's theories about how the world works. It keeps us (O'Connor argues in her "Introduction" to *A Memoir of Mary Ann*) from leaping to conclusions which betray us. It is a matter not of what we know, nor even of what we don't know, but only of whether we allow ourselves to claim that all the evidence is in. It is this skepticism which keeps us free — not free to do anything we please but free, as O'Connor wrote to Alfred Corn, to be formed by something larger than our own intellects or the intellects of those around us. Faith does not force us to abandon comprehension or to adopt a transparently false theory about why the world is as bad a place as it is, nor does it take comprehension to a place where it can comprehend the incomprehensible; faith takes comprehension to a place where, without compromising itself or falling into that mere error we call "the irrational," it recognizes that it is not master of what it surveys.

What faith has faith in remains hidden from us; it is something we sense only in our failure. It is because transcendence always presents itself as limitation, it is because we cannot represent transcendent things but only the difficulties they cause us and the incomprehension with which they leave us, that we cannot ever say with certainty, no matter what our inner certainties are, whether the author's intent is serious (to depict matters which escape depiction) or ironic (to depict our longing for experiences we cannot have). Irony and transfiguration are closely related in that they each draw an outer limit to language, and the reader's experience of that limit is the same regardless of which side the author seems to be on. Irony walks around the perimeter of language, marking its boundary with contradictions. But grace, standing on the other side of that same perimeter, seems to make use of the same contradictions. Resolution of this question probably depends more upon us than upon O'Connor. As with the Biblical parables (remarks John R. May) we do not interpret these stories, our reactions to them interpret us.

"The Capture" is a comedy about the impossibility of representing transcendence, but it is also a comedy about how the failure of the attempt to do so somehow brings the idea of transcendence home to us even while leaving us in acute doubt that we have really apprehended anything at all. If this early story is about the difficulty of representation, O'Connor's last story, "Parker's Back," is about the necessity of the attempt, and it approaches the limits described in "The Turkey" from the opposite direction.

The protagonist, O. E. Parker, is a dissatisfied man. He is dissatisfied with his severe, Straight Gospel wife, and more dissatisfied with himself for remaining with her or involving himself with her in the first place. (He seems to be a spectator of his own acts, not privy to his motivations and bewildered by his failure to act according to his acknowledged tastes.) Parker is also dissatisfied with the state of the tattoos which cover every part of his body other than his back, and which he feels ought to serve more than a decorative purpose. Here he also seems to be a spectator of his own actions—he knows that he has an obscure itch to get a new tattoo from time to time, but no new tattoo keeps him happy for long and their total effect is as haphazard and unsatisfactory as his marriage.

Parker first became interested in tattoos when, at the age of fourteen, he saw a man tattooed from head to foot in a sideshow. The moment O'Connor describes here is related to the moment in *Wise Blood* when Hazel Motes, at a similar age, saw a naked woman in a casket in a sideshow, and failing to see a sign from God after he had walked with sharp rocks in his shoes as a penance, began to conclude that there is no God. It is also related to another moment in a sideshow, the appearance of the hermaphrodite in "A Temple of the Holy Ghost." These sideshows seem to be places where large decisions are made, places where religion is gained or lost—as if their grotesquerie demonstrated the results O'Connor expected her own grotesques to have.

Whether this moment is more closely related to the one in *Wise Blood* or to the one in "A Temple of the Holy Ghost" is not at first clear. The tattooed man himself is described reverently, like the hermaphrodite, and the designs upon his body seem to express the ability of signs of nature to represent a radiance and wholeness which is almost religious in character:

> The man's skin was patterned in what seemed from Parker's distance
> —he was near the back of the tent, standing on a bench—a single
> intricate design of brilliant color. The man, who was small and

sturdy, moved about on the platform, flexing his muscles so that the arabesque of men and beasts and flowers on his skin appeared to have a subtle motion of its own.

O'Connor describes Parker's reaction, however, in terms which deflate the description they follow: "Parker was filled with emotion, lifted up as some people are when the flag passes." If we have been tempted to look upon the "arabesque of men and beasts and flowers" as natural symbols expressing God's majesty, this next sentence makes fools of us. Parker here seems to become a sort of Enoch Emery, full of foolish and vulgar enthusiasms which crudely take the place of inspiration, and the story seems to represent his fascination with beasts and with his wise blood, or Ruby Hill's fascination with astrology in "A Stroke of Good Fortune"—merely an example of the debased forms to which the spirit turns when it denies religion to itself.

But Parker, for all of the many tattoos he acquires in the midst of his random experiences in the Navy and in jail, never finds his tattoos to be a source of lasting satisfaction:

> Wherever a decent-sized mirror was available, he would get in front of it and study his overall look. The effect was not of one intricate arabesque of colors but of something haphazard and botched. A huge dissatisfaction would come over him and he would go off and find another tattooist and have another space filled up.

This dissatisfaction raises Parker a little in our eyes—we see him as hungering for something of which he cannot form a clear idea and as honest enough to recognize the inadequacy of his expedients, and we begin to honor his hunger as a disguised hunger for higher things of which we can as yet form no explicit idea.

It is this same dissatisfaction which leads him, to his own puzzlement, to marry Sarah Ruth Cates. We first see her as we last see her, swinging a broom at Parker. Fixing his truck in front of her house and sensing the pressure of female eyes upon his back, he pretends to have hurt his hand and jumps about, swearing, in order to draw her attention to his tattoos. She hits him over the head with her broom on account of his language, and will have none of his vanities (she even refers to the eagle on his hand as a chicken). What leads Parker to marry her—immediately after he has decided to have nothing to do with her—is exactly her dislike of his tattoos, for it seems to be a reflected form of his own discontent. It is, as he sees it, as if she could see through him (although she doesn't), as if she could look down from above on the flimsiness of his artifices and could rest secure in the possession of that obscure thing which Parker mistakenly looks for in the tattooing parlor.

Satisfying Sarah Ruth and converting the haphazard patchwork on his skin into a flowing arabesque gradually become related problems. The same dim promptings which led him to the tattoo parlor and to the County Ordinary's office at length begin to urge him to put a tattoo with a religious subject on his back, solving both his problems in one stroke. After a symbolically loaded accident—he rams his employer's tractor into a tree, shouting "GOD ABOVE!" as he is propelled out of his seat and away from the flaming branches—he drives to the city, feeling that a great and inexplicable change has happened in his life, and has his back tattooed with the image of "a flat stern Byzantine Christ with all-demanding eyes" which his wise blood, crying out "go back" as he thumbed past it in the tattooist's picture book, had forced him to choose.

His enthusiasm spent after two days under the tattooist's hand and an uneasy night at the Haven of Light Christian Mission, Parker, embarrassed at revealing his new tattoo to his drinking buddies and angrily denying that he's "got religion and is witnessing for Jesus" (although in fact that seems to be just what he is doing), gets involved in a drunken brawl. Examining his soul afterward, he sees it as "a spider web of facts and lies that was not at all important to him but which appeared to be necessary in spite of his opinion," and returns to Sarah Ruth, hoping that his new tattoo will mollify her. He finds his door locked, and his wife refusing to open it until he utters his true name, Obadiah Elihue. At that instant the sun rises, a "tree of light" bursts over the horizon, and Parker falls back against the door "as if he had been pinned there by a lance," feeling the light "pouring through him, turning his spider web soul into a perfect arabesque of colors, a garden of trees and birds and beasts."

The moment is a parodic epiphany, but we take it seriously anyway, for this arabesque is painted for us in all the colors of redemption. In fact, the very openness to ridicule of Parker's act becomes grounds for taking it seriously when we recognize that among the burdens of this story is the demonstration of how enlightenment, because it must always come in unexpected ways, must always look like something else, something false or embarrassing. Parker's vision, improvised, pathetic, apparently ruled out in advance, seems ridiculous only because all vision must seem to be so, otherwise it would not be vision but perception.

When Sarah Ruth beats Parker with her broom, screaming that his new tattoo is idolatrous, and that God is a spirit whom no man shall see, our sympathies are entirely with poor Parker, and our judgment is that Sarah Ruth is wrong not only about her husband's motives but also about God. But her error is precisely the error the narrator of "The Turkey" seems to drive us into. If catching a turkey is no sign that God considers you an "unusual child," then having a tattoo is no satisfactory way of "witnessing for Christ" and the transformation Parker feels standing on his doorstep is so much moonshine. The stories seem to repeal each

other, for either we can comprehend God through symbols or we cannot. Like
Ruller, we are absolutely shut out of the secret of the story, and like Parker, we
are beaten from pillar to post.

II

The governing assumption of our two stories is that transcendence cannot
be reckoned with either through propositions (which give one only philosophy)
or through symbols (which give one only idolatry). The consequence of this assumption is that the stories waver, in restless discontent, between two mutually
exclusive and equally untenable positions, between the claim that when one attempts to represent transcendence one necessarily creates only a ridiculously inflated and unwittingly parodic picture of one's own self, and the claim that
transcendence itself demands representation in practical terms even in the face
of the recognition that no symbol, and no course of life, can do it justice. It is
this wavering which is the closest thing O'Connor provides to a representation of
transcendence, for it enacts the restlessness and discontent which are the portion
of those who would grapple with the intractability of an ultimate concern.

A God whom we can comprehend inevitably becomes an idol, but a God
whom we cannot comprehend inevitably becomes nothing. The agnostic and
the orthodox come together on the question of God's mystery, and the agnostic's
restlessness in the grip of a desperate spiritual problem is markedly similar to the
believer's restlessness in the grip of a spiritual demand. Both figures join in
Hazel Motes of *Wise Blood*, whose atheism is, in a strange way, his half-con-
scious testimony to the strength of his baffled belief in an utterly unknowable
God.

The story of how *Wise Blood* rebukes Hazel Motes' atheism, and how he
comes to see the error and failure of the beliefs which identify him, has been
much discussed already. But the real story of *Wise Blood* is not just about how
Hazel is wrong—else the novel could have been simply a longer "The Life You
Save May Be Your Own" with Enoch Emery and Hoover Shoats as main characters. Hazel does parody Existentialism, and insofar as he does this, he is a figure
of fun. But he is not only a figure of fun, and if we take him at all seriously we do
so not because O'Connor has secret atheist sensibilities which cause her to take
his side unbeknownst to herself but because he also has a sort of integrity about
which O'Connor is very much in earnest. Hazel is wrong, and sometimes he is
wrong and silly. Where he is not silly, he is wrong as Ahab is wrong; his errors are
part of his dramatic power and their fascination is a consequence of their resemblance to the difficulties of the author's own position. In his way Hazel shares,
this is to say, the spiritual predicament of his author; but even more Hazel shares

her power. Both juxtapose two similar but irreconcilable things, the restlessness and destructive impatience enjoined upon them by their hunger for ultimate truths, and the power that restlessness confers upon those who embrace it, the power to resist all determinations and become in one's self as mysterious and as intractable and as gleefully destructive as that mystery to which one is subject. Haze represents, in short, the originating power of the author's imagination, the power to create discontinuities and to solicit incomprehension; in his fate we see the inherent dangers of that power.

We define this power negatively—it is the power to reject determinations and to hold the case open when it appears to be closed. It has the strength of rejection, not the strength of affirmation. It is fitting then that Haze is described to us in terms of what he lacks rather than in terms of what he is. We do not see him as a character at rest in a society in which he has a place, but as a displaced person who, after returning from four years in the army to the hamlet which had been his home and finding that it has disappeared, is on his way to a city where he knows nobody.

It is a commonplace that American romancers—and O'Connor explicitly calls herself one—do not describe characters by describing their place in the social or familial world they inhabit but by describing what obsession or what circumstances have caused them not to do what everybody else does. We begin with a catastrophic external event, the self-identification of the character as a wanderer or the adoption of an obsession which marks him off as different in kind from the other characters and frees him, at least in his own eyes, from the standards of judgment applied to those characters. It is the strenuousness of Haze's rejections which most characterize him, bestowing upon him through the very tenacity with which he makes them, an integrity which survives, and is meant to survive, his author's continual ridicule of him.

Haze's rejections are derived, however, from two prior failures. As a child he had slipped into a sideshow where a naked woman was on display; his father was in the audience. Were it not for the humor which constantly undercuts the scene in an attempt to prevent us from taking Haze seriously, we might call it a classic initiation into sin, death, sex, and the fallibility of authority. Afterwards, suffering not only the guilt for this specific sin but the same nameless unplaced guilt which will lead him to a similar course of action at the end of the novel (when he has more to repent of), he filled his shoes with sharp stones and waited for a sign from God which never came. It was a powerful disappointment. Like Tarwater at a similar age, and like Satan in the temptations (or like Jonah), he wanted to give law to God, and he felt that God had made a fool of him by not behaving as he expected him to; it is an error to which too much faith, as well as too little, is liable.

The second failure came after several years during which he had tried to avoid the wild ragged figure of Jesus by avoiding sin and keeping his feet always on the known track, when he found himself in the army and felt as lost as if he had been walking on water unawares. When some friends asked him to go with them to a brothel, he put on his mother's glasses (which he also wears toward the end of the novel during a similar moment of moral severity, when he destroys the "new jesus") and delivered a moralizing speech. It earned him only laughter. What was particularly humiliating to him here was that his attempt to keep his virtue appeared to have no reward. After being sent to several deserts, in which in Cartesian parody, he studied his soul until he convinced himself that it didn't exist, he set out, on being discharged, to preach the Church Without Christ.

Both of these moments are moments of failure and humiliation, moments when Haze is deprived of what he might have relied upon. But by seizing on what thwarts him, Haze turns a moment of limitation into one of origination. Haze creates himself by standing against the principles which might otherwise have defined him. Identification with what had limited and humiliated one seems to transform one into something larger than one's self (since one stands outside of one's self). It makes one something which always eludes the grasp of comprehension since, being founded on negation and denial of what one was, rather than on any positive principle, it gives comprehension nothing to grasp. Haze has a purely negative power—like Milton's Satan—a power to resist, to overturn, to deny, and to perplex, a power which resembles the power of the author and which, like the author's power, expresses itself, and is called forth, by means of limitation and incomprehension.

Where characters assume this negative power, even the facts we know about them do not define them. We know Haze only by what he has lost. We know every job the Misfit in "A Good Man Is Hard to Find" has ever had, but we never feel that those jobs place him, and the list seems to be a compilation of attributes which pointedly fail to define him, an exhaustive but unsatisfactory description of the things he might have been but did not remain. All we know about the Misfit is that he founds his selfhood — and even takes his name from — his inabilities: his inability to make what he has suffered fit with what he has done, and his inability to decide whether Jesus really did raise the dead. A selfhood we know positively is defined by and limited by its characterizing attributes. A selfhood founded on a limitation or absence seems to escape us. By identifying himself with a limiting power, by accepting only negative definitions, the character seems to stand on the other side of this defining limitation, to become unlimited himself however limited our ability to comprehend him may be.

Haze is partly mistaken about the nature of his own rejections. He believes that he has been "converted to nothing instead of to evil," and he forms his "Church Without Christ" to spread a doctrine which his hearers — as he hilariously fails to see — already believe more thoroughly than he does. Those who are really converted to nothing instead of to evil, this is to say, are not strenuous rejectors like Haze but foolish materialists like Hoover Shoats. What Haze's rejections really amount to can be described in two ways.

Partly one must say that Haze's rejection is not a settled doctrine but a tense and continuous holding off of a belief he is too inwardly wise to finally let go of, that his energy and inwardness is the energy and inwardness of the transcendence he resists. This reading explains why Haze keeps looking for a worthy opponent to prove himself against — what he thinks he finds in Hawks — and explains also why he so violently rejects characters like Enoch Emery, Hoover Shoats, and Solace Layfield, who parodically reflect him, and who, in fact, believe what he spends all his energy attempting to believe. The mystery of Hazel's selfhood is a sort of reflected version of the mystery of God. Haze's "Church Without Christ" has the shape of the evangelical faith it is an attempt to repudiate because his own selfhood depends in crucial ways upon the religion he denies and makes himself into himself by denying.

This first formulation, although authorized by O'Connor herself and repeated by almost all of her critics, seems to me to account for only a part of Haze's power. For his magnetism as a character and his redemption as a person do not arise from some inner reservation he holds about his rejections but from the very doggedness with which he persists in trying to maintain them. Haze's "Church Without Christ" represents a genuine, although perverse, attempt to wrestle with serious spiritual questions which his repudiations force him to face in an unmediated way and which settled and complacent belief might have allowed him to duck. What I mean to say here is that Haze's rejections do not take him out of the religious sphere but are instead versions of the act central to the whole Judeo-Christian tradition, the rejection of idolatry, the rejection of the notion that God is comprehensible and can be reckoned with. Haze wears the same face Abraham wore when he smashed his father's idols in Ur, and his repudiation of all religion whatsoever is only the logical culmination of Abraham's act, even though he himself does not realize this until the end of the book. The thoroughgoing destroyer of idols, this is to say, can only sound like the perfect atheist, and only his dramatic power proves him to be anything other. Only the fact that Haze himself remains a mystery confirms the fact that he continues to face one, even if he has destroyed the language in which that mystery might be defined. Haze's repudiations do not leave him in an empty secular world; they leave him facing, with no compromising mediations, two related, unwordable, and equally mysterious imperatives, "I," and "the Abyss."

This view of Hazel Motes has two consequences concerning Flannery O'Connor as a religious novelist. The first is that David Eggenschwiler and Miles Orvell and many others are correct in arguing that O'Connor's inspiration is fundamentally religious and that her aim is persuasion concerning religious matters. The second is that Carol Shloss and Peter Hawkins are also correct in arguing that her works are incapable of conveying particular religious doctrines, and that the shocks they administer to the reader are not, as O'Connor herself described them, the large and startling figures one must draw for the nearly spiritually blind if one is to get one's point across, but are rather instances of that inscrutability and dark comedy which has been the burden of fiction since Kafka and Nathanael West and which we traditionally associate with a wrought-up atheism. Where Shloss and Hawkins are wrong is that they believe that this experience of disorientation and horror is not itself religious. In fact, unmediated horror, and especially unmediated horror which cannot be contained in certain rationalizations concerning God's ultimate benevolence, has always been the central fact of religious experience, the experience of Isaac, of Job, and of Jesus. What O'Connor's works present the reader with is not a body of illustrated doctrine, nor even a body of doctrine hammered with ruthless irony into the minds of recalcitrant readers, but the experience of doubt about whether life has any meaning at all, an experience which religion exists to enlarge, not to pacify. That God is so inscrutable that he disappears at crucial moments and lets no faith in him rest in comfort, that nature and fate are so incomprehensible and so violent that we cannot hope to grasp them, only to bear them as bravely as we can, is not an atheistic thought; on the contrary, it is the thought to which any religion that is not a tissue of rationalizations and wishful thinking must perpetually return.

What sort of religion can be founded on such denials, can be a Church Without Christ? When Haze presents himself at the door of Mrs. Flood as a minister of the Church Without Christ, she asks him suspiciously whether That church is Protestant or Catholic. No Mam, replies Haze, it is Protestant. O'Connor intends this as a sectarian dig against "atheists of Protestant traditions," and she means by it the familiar argument that the Reformation was the first step in the vaporization of religion. She remarks in a letter to Ben Griffith dated March 3, 1954 that *Wise Blood* "reduces Protestantism to the twin ultimate absurdities of the Church Without Christ or the Holy Church of Christ Without Christ." In this same letter, however, she refers to Haze without irony as "a kind of Protestant saint," because his nihilism, instead of leading him into Rayber-like secularism or Hoover Shoats-like opportunism, "leads him back to the fact of his Redemption, however, which is what he would have liked so much to get away from."

Haze's affinities seem to be as much with the Protestant prophets he repudiates as with the atheists whose beliefs he shares but who lack his vitality. His rejection of belief is not the washed-out post-Christianity of Hulga or Rayber, but a powerful inward, almost Gnostic rejection, a wrestling with belief like that Tarwater goes through in *The Violent Bear It Away;* it is related to the no less incomprehensible inward powers of the believers, although it is open at both ends (as O'Connor says of Protestantism), to belief and to unbelief. The inward power to which Haze lays claim through rejection is similar in nature to that claimed by the Protestant prophets, for the defining movement in Protestantism has always been to replace identifiable external sources of authority and standards of judgment with mysterious internal authorities, rejecting first the authority of the Pope, then the authority of the Bishops, then the clergy, and finally every authority other than the inner light. Hazel Motes represents the most radical form of Protestantism, a Protestantism which overthrows the authority of God as much as it overthrows the authority of the clergy, all in the name of a spirit which becomes more vacant as it becomes more pure, until belief in nothing but the spirit, belief in nothing, and belief in nothing but oneself, become indistinguishable.

To reject every authority but wise blood is to run certain very large risks. Purely internal authorities easily become on one hand the dim promptings of instinct, as they do for Enoch Emery (who seems to be the originator of the phrase "wise blood") or on the other hand, a warm bath of comfortable sentiments, as they do, if not for Hoover Shoats, at least for his would-be disciples. In the absence of a public institution to govern the interpretation it becomes difficult to decide whether what one obscurely feels is the misery of original sin or simply the vapors; the rejection of external authority leaves the character of the internal authority which replaces it indeterminate. The problem of Protestantism and the problem of the authority of the imagination, then, are linked. As O'Connor said of Old Tarwater (in a letter to William Sessions dated September 29, 1960):

> When the Protestant hears what he supposes to be the voice of the Lord, he follows it regardless of whether it runs counter to the Church's teaching. The Catholic believes any voice he may hear may come from the Devil unless it is in accordance with the teachings of the Church.

What results when this process of rejection is pushed to its limit is that belief and unbelief begin to look like each other and the claims of both escape us. It is fitting that Enoch's wise blood should lead him to worship a mummy and that Haze's visions should all be about premature burial. For we cannot decide whether a purely negative idea of transcendence can transcend its denials. Poe, following a related course, describes his motivation as a "wild longing for the Beauty Above," but in his similarly motivated characters this longing seems chiefly to result in ghoulish hocus-pocus: Usher makes his sister a spirit by burying her alive, and the narrator of "Ligeia" recaptures his lost love, if not by actual murder, at least by some sort of necromancy. When one purifies sense by rejecting it, when one makes language transcendent by emptying it of reference and makes women spiritual by emptying them of life, one's achievements are always equivocal and look (and may even ultimately be) not only failures but grotesque parodies of the success they strive for. These are the risks which the characters face. They are also the risks to which authors attracted to similar negative means are subject.

O'Connor answers this danger by not fully identifying with Haze. The function of her continual undermining and undercutting of Haze is not to make him look ridiculous—for she is not entirely successful in doing so—but to separate her point of view from his. She is interested in Protestants, but she herself remains a Catholic, and what she understands as the stability of Catholic tradition allows her to distance herself from the vicissitudes of Protestant wise blood even while she relies upon it as not only the subject but also the motive power of the novel. She pokes fun at Haze (principally through presenting a parody of him in Enoch but also by undercutting him directly) and is thus able to avoid suffering the consequences of internal power which Haze suffers. The distance her judgments (and the humor which reflects those judgments) place between her and Haze allows her to stand apart from unspoken authorial claims of inward authority very like Haze's own. She uses Catholicism to tame Protestantism just as Hawthorne claims to use Realism to tame Romance. *Wise Blood* represents a transaction between Haze and herself, between an internal and therefore undefinable power, and a definable external control. In "The Catholic Novelist in the Protestant South" she describes what the Catholic has to offer the world of these powers, the world at once of Protestantism and of American Romance, this way:

> In a literature that tends naturally to extremes, as Southern literature
> does, we need something to protect us against the merely extreme,
> the merely personal, the merely grotesque, and here the Catholic,
> with his older tradition and his ability to resist the dissolution of
> belief, can make his contribution to Southern literature, but only if
> he realizes that he has as much to learn from it as to give it.

O'Connor does not, however, use this transaction to control Haze. Haze remains himself, and even at the end of the novel he is not altered. His salvation works itself out using the same means his nihilism had already used; he is not stopped or restrained by the author. What O'Connor uses her Catholicism to restrain is not Haze but herself. It is easy enough to see how Haze might have been overthrown. He might easily have been made to suffer the fate—simultaneously discrediting and transforming—of her many farm widows. He could suffer the fate of Hulga Hopewell of "Good Country People," to be reduced to the laughing-stock he has always threatened to become and which Enoch Emery always was. In fact, he could have been overthrown simply by being made to go through all of the things he actually does suffer (and inflict upon himself) in the last pages of the novel.

As O'Connor had said to Hulga "This is what comes of believing in nothing," so she might have said to Haze, "This is what comes of wise blood, this is the sort of lunacy you commit yourself to when you throw out every authority but inward ones which can as easily be moonshine as truth." In fact, O'Connor deliberately leaves open the possibility that Haze is after all just a case of deviant psychology, for his final penances are simply reversions to the self-punishments he had inflicted upon himself when he was a guilty child. We might describe the whole course of action as Rayber would describe young Tarwater's, as a rebellion directed against a powerful, religious paternal authority but which imitates the methods of that authority (Haze, like his grandfather, preaches from the nose of his car), and which collapses into guilt and penances which that authority might have dictated. But it is no more satisfactory to write off Haze as a deviant than it is to write off Hawthorne's madmen as deviants, for we cannot do so without doubting whether they are sane after all, and whether our psychology is really only a set of defensive illusions.

Haze not only is not discredited by his penances, he is actually raised in our eyes. He is not overthrown at all by the restraining power of O'Connor's judgments. In fact, she seems to be the one who goes to meet him, for it is in his terms, not hers, that his salvation is worked out. The things he suffers, which might have been punishment, seem in the author's eyes to become a variety of martyrdom, as if the very wise blood which led him astray could lead him back also. As O'Connor wrote to Hawkes on 13 September 1959:

> Haze is saved by virtue of having wise blood, it's too wise for him ultimately to deny Christ. Wise blood has to be these people's means of grace—they have no sacraments. The religion of the South is a do-it-yourself religion, something which I as a Catholic find painful and touching and grimly comic. It's full of unconscious pride that lands them in all sorts of ridiculous religious predicaments. They have nothing to correct their practical heresies and so they work them out dramatically. If this were merely comic to me, it would be no good, but I accept the same fundamental doctrines of sin and redemption and judgment that they do.

Far from becoming a figure of fun, Haze becomes an example of the traditional holy sinner, with his nihilism being the very sin that leads him to God.
Haze could have been saved by being made to reject his wise blood. But instead
he seems to deny his way through to the other side of his denials. His redemption is the natural consequence of his sin, and his wise blood, at which the
novelist set out to scoff, becomes, almost against her will, something of which
she is a little in awe.

To turn against one's self as Haze does — at once punishing and transcending that self — is something one can only do in the name of a larger and darker
self established by that very act of self-rejection. The poet who rejects his own
skill, for example, does so in the name of his muse, and the muse, although
always other than the poet we recognize, represents a seat of poetic identity
deeper than the poet's own wishes, skill, or knowledge. In an identical way Haze
humbles and destroys the self we know, but as he does so he honors an unseen
self which is established by his very act of humiliation. Like the poet, he rejects
himself and becomes himself in the same gesture, and like the poet he also cannot finally tell whether the self he becomes is a yet more monstrous inflation of
himself, or whether it is instead the image of the participation of the intimate
mystery of selfhood in the final mystery of God. Haze does not destroy himself;
he escapes us, still clearly himself, but now a self which seems beyond anything
we recognize as selfhood:

> The outline of a skull was plain under his skin and the deep burned
> eye sockets seemed to lead into the dark tunnel where he had disap-
> peared. (Mrs. Flood) leaned closer and closer to his face, looking
> deep into them, trying to see how she had been cheated or what had
> cheated her, but she couldn't see anything. She shut her eyes and
> saw the pin point of light but so far away that she could not hold it
> steady in her mind. She felt as if she were blocked at the entrance of
> something. She sat staring with her eyes shut, into his eyes, and felt
> as if she had finally got to the beginning of something she couldn't
> begin, and she saw him moving farther and farther away, farther
> and farther into the darkness until he was the pin point of light.

What Haze does is simply to live through the consequences of his errors
with integrity. As he had, in the beginning of the novel, appropriated a failure
and founded himself by doing so, so when his nihilism fails him he appropriates
that failure and transcends himself a second time. In both cases, it is the inward
power we associate with the romance character which drives him, for in both
cases it is not what he does but what he fails to do which defines his integrity.
When O'Connor in her introductory note to *Wise Blood* proclaims that our

integrity lies in what we are not able to do, what she has in mind is precisely this integrity—integrity severe enough to press its project to its logical conclusion, candid enough to recognize when that conclusion has come to pieces, and large enough to honor that thing beyond itself with which failure faces it. Haze's mystery is more even than this; it is that the integrity with which he owns his error and the integrity with which he makes it are not finally two different things. Haze's recognition is not that he was wrong about God but that his very repudiation of God was a way of testifying to his mystery. Finally we cannot distinguish Haze's piety from his impiety, his experience of grace from his punishment.

O'Connor has it both ways in *Wise Blood.* She herself rejects the inward power which her characters take as their sole authority, and through irony and even ridicule she forcefully keeps her point of view separate from theirs. But at the same time this inward power seems not only to redeem Haze but to win him the grudging respect of both author and reader, as if by failing strenuously he could convert the failure a more ironic author would have imposed upon him into a kind of success. O'Connor allows herself both of the alternatives she ruled out in "The Turkey" and "Parker's Back." The novel leaves her and Haze in a perilous but acutely balanced standoff.

Chronology

1925   Mary Flannery O'Connor born to Edward F. and Regina O'Connor on March 25, in Savannah, Georgia.

1938   Family moves to Milledgeville, Georgia.

1941   Father dies of lupus.

1945   Graduates from Georgia State College for Women.

1945–48   Attends Writer's Workshop at State University of Iowa. M.F.A. 1947. "The Geranium" published in 1946 in *Accent*.

1949   Lives in New York City. Chapters from *Wise Blood* published in *Partisan Review*. Goes to live with Sally and Robert Fitzgerald in Connecticut.

1950   Suffers first attack of lupus in December. While she will be able, by the use of drugs, to control the disease somewhat, it will eventually kill her.

1951   Returns to Milledgeville, where last years are spent.

1952   *Wise Blood* published.

1953   Kenyon Fellowship.

1954   "The Life You Save May Be Your Own" awarded second prize in the O. Henry awards for short stories.

1955   *A Good Man Is Hard to Find* published. "A Circle in the Fire" wins second prize in the O. Henry awards. From this time on, O'Connor must use crutches.

1957   "Greenleaf" wins first prize in O. Henry awards. O'Connor receives National Institute of Arts and Letters grant.

1958   Travels to Lourdes and Rome, accompanied by her mother. Audience with the Pope.

1959   Receives a Ford Foundation grant.

1960   *The Violent Bear It Away* published.

1963   "Everything That Rises Must Converge" awarded first prize in O. Henry awards.

1964   Dies on August 3 in Milledgeville Hospital. "Revelation" wins first prize in O. Henry awards.

1971   *The Complete Stories of Flannery O'Connor* wins National Book Award.

Contributors

HAROLD BLOOM, Sterling Professor of the Humanities at Yale University, is the author of *The Anxiety of Influence, Poetry and Repression*, and many other volumes of literary criticism. His forthcoming study, *Freud: Transference and Authority*, attempts a full-scale reading of all of Freud's major writings. A MacArthur Prize Fellow, he is general editor of five series of literary criticism published by Chelsea House.

JOHN HAWKES, novelist and critic, is Professor of English at Brown University. Among his best-known novels are *The Cannibal, Second Skin,* and *Death, Sleep, and the Traveler*. His most recent book is *Adventures in the Alaska Skin Trade*.

ROBERT FITZGERALD, poet and translator, is best known for his translations of the *Iliad* and the *Odyssey*. His last translation was a beautiful rendering of the *Aeneid*.

LEWIS A. LAWSON is Professor of English at the University of Maryland. He is co-editor of *The Added Dimension: The Mind and Art of Flannery O'Connor*.

JOYCE CAROL OATES is a novelist whose best-known works include *Wonderland, Childwold,* and *Son of the Morning*. The author of numerous critical essays, she teaches in the Department of Creative Writing at Princeton University.

RALPH C. WOOD is Professor of Religious Studies at Wake Forest University.

CAROL SHLOSS is the author of *Flannery O'Connor's Dark Comedies*.

RONALD SCHLEIFER is Associate Professor of English at the University of Oklahoma. He is the editor of *The Genres of the Irish Literary Revival*.

FREDERICK ASALS is Associate Professor of English at the University of Toronto. He is the author of *Flannery O'Connor: The Imagination of Extremity*. JEFFERSON HUMPHRIES is Assistant Professor of French at Louisiana State University, and is the author of *The Otherness Within*.

JOHN BURT is Assistant Professor of English at Brandeis University. He has published articles on Woolf, O'Connor, and American Romantic fiction, and will soon be publishing a book on Robert Penn Warren.

Bibliography

Alice, Sister Rose, S. S. J. "Flannery O'Connor: Poet to the Outcast." *Renascence* 16 (1964): 126–32.

Asals, Frederick. *Flannery O'Connor: The Imagination of Extremity.* Athens: University of Georgia Press, 1982.

———. "The Mythic Dimensions of Flannery O'Connor's 'Greenleaf.'" *Studies in Short Fiction* 5 (1968): 317–30.

———. "The Road to *Wise Blood.*" *Renascence* 21 (1969): 181–94.

Bassan, Maurice. "Flannery O'Connor's Way: Shock, with Moral Intent." *Renascence* 15 (1963): 195–99, 211.

Baumbach, Jonathan. *The Landscape of Nightmare.* New York: New York University Press, 1965.

Brinkmeyer, Robert H., Jr. "Borne Away by Violence: The Reader and Flannery O'Connor." *Southern Review* 15 (1979): 313–21.

Browning, Preston. *Flannery O'Connor.* Carbondale: Southern Illinois University Press, 1964.

Burns, Stuart L. "Flannery O'Connor's Literary Apprenticeship." *Renascence* 22 (1969): 3–16.

Carlson, Thomas M. "Flannery O'Connor: The Manichean Dilemma." *Sewanee Review* 77 (1969): 254–76.

Coles, Robert. *Flannery O'Connor's South.* Baton Rouge: Louisiana State University Press, 1980.

Desmond, John F. "The Shifting of Mr. Shiftlet: Flannery O'Connor's 'The Life You Save May Be Your Own.'" *Mississippi Quarterly* 28 (1975): 55–59.

Drake, Robert. *Flannery O'Connor.* Grand Rapids: Wm. B. Erdmans, 1966.

Driskell, Leon, and Joan Brittain. *The External Crossroads: The Art of Flannery O'Connor.* Lexington: University of Kentucky Press, 1971.

Edelstein, Mark G. "Flannery O'Connor and the Problem of Modern Satire." *Studies in Short Fiction* 12 (1975): 139–44.

Eggenschwiler, David. *The Christian Humanism of Flannery O'Connor.* Detroit: Wayne State University Press, 1972.

Esprit 8 (Winter 1964). Special Flannery O'Connor issue.

Feeley, Kathleen. *Flannery O'Connor: The Voice of the Peacock.* New Brunswick, N.J.: Rutgers University Press, 1972.

Feeley, Margaret Peller. "Flannery O'Connor's *Wise Blood:* The Negative Way." *Southern Quarterly* 17 (1979): 104–22.

The Flannery O'Connor Bulletin. Milledgeville, Ga. 1972–.

Friedman, Melvin, and Lewis A. Lawson, eds. *The Added Dimension: The Mind and Art of Flannery O'Connor.* New York: Fordham University Press, 1966.

Gordon, Caroline. "Heresy in Dixie." *Sewanee Review* 76 (1968): 263–97.

Guerard, Albert J., ed. *Stories of the Double.* Philadelphia: J. B. Lippincott, 1967.

Hawkins, Peter S. *The Language of Grace: Flannery O'Connor, Walker Percy, and Iris Murdoch.* Cambridge, Mass.: Cowley Publications, 1983.

Hendlin, Josephine. *The World of Flannery O'Connor.* Bloomington: University of Indiana Press, 1970.

Humphries, Jefferson. *The Otherness Within: Gnostic Readings in Proust, Flannery O'Connor, and François Villon.* Baton Rouge: Louisiana State University Press, 1983.

Hyman, Stanley Edgar. *Flannery O'Connor.* Minneapolis: University of Minnesota Press, 1966.

Kahane, Claire. "Artificial Niggers." *Massachusetts Review* 19 (1978): 183–98.

Katz, Claire. "Flannery O'Connor's Rage of Vision." *American Literature* 46 (1974–75): 54–67.

Koon, William. " 'Hep Me Not to Be So Mean': Flannery O'Connor's Subjectivity." *Southern Review* 15 (1979): 322–32.

Martin, Carter W. *The True Country: Themes in the Fiction of Flannery O'Connor.* Nashville: Vanderbilt University Press, 1968.

———. "Flannery O'Connor's Early Fiction." *Southern Humanities Review* 7 (1973): 210–14.

May, John R. *The Pruning Word: The Parables of Flannery O'Connor.* Notre Dame, Ind.: Notre Dame University Press, 1976.

McDermott, John V. "O'Connor's 'A Stroke of Good Fortune.' " *Explicator* 38, no. 4 (1980): 13–14.

Milder, Robert. "The Protestantism of Flannery O'Connor." *Southern Review* 11 (1975): 802–19.

Montgomery, Marion. "The Artist as 'A Very Doubtful Jacob': A Reflection on Hawthorne and O'Connor." *Southern Quarterly* 16 (1978): 95–103.

———. "Flannery O'Connor and the Jansenist Problem in Fiction." *Southern Review* 14 (1978): 438–48.

Muller, Gilbert H. *Nightmares and Visions: Flannery O'Connor and the Catholic Grotesque.* Athens: University of Georgia Press, 1972.

Nisly, Paul W. "The Prison of Self: Isolation in Flannery O'Connor's Fiction." *Studies in Short Fiction* 17 (1980): 49–54.

Orvell, Miles. *Invisible Parade: The Fiction of Flannery O'Connor.* Philadelphia: Temple University Press, 1972.

Rechnitz, Robert M. "Passionate Pilgrim: Flannery O'Connor's *Wise Blood.*" *Georgia Review* 19 (1965): 310–16.

Reiter, Robert, ed. *Flannery O'Connor.* St. Louis: B. Herder, 1968.

Renascence 22, no. 1 (Autumn 1969). Special Flannery O'Connor issue.

Shear, Walter. "Flannery O'Connor: Character and Characterization." *Renascence* 20 (1968): 140–46.

Shloss, Carol. *Flannery O'Connor's Dark Comedies: The Limits of Inference.* Baton Rouge: Louisiana State University Press, 1980.

Stevens, Martha. *The Question of Flannery O'Connor.* Baton Rouge: Louisiana State University Press, 1973.

Tate, J. O. "Flannery O'Connor's Counterplot." *Southern Review* 16 (1980): 869–78.

Van de Kieft, Ruth. "Judgment in Flannery O'Connor." *Sewanee Review* 76 (1968): 337–56.

Walters, Dorothy. *Flannery O'Connor.* New York: Twayne, 1973.

Acknowledgments

"Flannery O'Connor's Devil" by John Hawkes from *Sewanee Review* 70, no. 3 (July–September 1962), © 1962 by the University of the South. Reprinted by permission of the editor of *Sewanee Review*.

"The Countryside and the True Country" by Robert Fitzgerald from *Sewanee Review* 70, no. 3 (July–September 1962), © 1962 by the University of the South. Reprinted by permission of the editor of the *Sewanee Review*.

"*Everything That Rises Must Converge*" (originally entitled "Introduction") by Robert Fitzgerald from *Everything That Rises Must Converge* by Flannery O'Connor, © 1956, 1957, 1958, 1960, 1961, 1962, 1964, 1965 by the Estate of Mary Flannery O'Connor. Reprinted by permission of Farrar, Straus and Giroux.

"The Perfect Deformity: *Wise Blood*" (originally entitled "Flannery O'Connor and the Grotesque: *Wise Blood*") by Lewis A. Lawson from *Renascence: Essays on Values in Literature* 17, no. 2 (Spring 1965), © 1964 by Catholic Renascence Society, Inc. Reprinted by permission.

"The Visionary Art of Flannery O'Connor" by Joyce Carol Oates from *Southern Humanities Review* 7, no. 3 (Summer 1973), © 1973 by *Southern Humanities Review*, Auburn University, Auburn, Ala. Reprinted by permission.

"From Fashionable Tolerance to Unfashionable Redemption" (originally entitled "From Fashionable Tolerance to Unfashionable Redemption: A Reading of Flannery O'Connor's First and Last Stories") by Ralph C. Wood from *The Flannery O'Connor Bulletin* 7 (Autumn 1978), © 1978 by *The Flannery O'Connor Bulletin*, Georgia College. Reprinted by permission.

"Epiphany" by Carol Shloss from *Flannery O'Connor's Dark Comedies: The Limits of Inference* by Carol Shloss, © 1980 by Louisiana State University Press. Reprinted by permission of the publisher.

"Rural Gothic" (originally entitled "Rural Gothic: The Stories of Flannery O'Connor") by Ronald Schleifer from *Modern Fiction Studies* 28, no. 3 (Autumn 1982), © 1982 by the Purdue Research Foundation, West Lafayette, Ind. Reprinted by permission.

"The Double" by Frederick Asals from *Flannery O'Connor: The Imagination of Extremity* by Frederick Asals, © 1982 by the University of Georgia Press. Reprinted by permission of the publisher.

"Proust, Flannery O'Connor, and the Aesthetic of Violence" by Jefferson Humphries from *The Otherness Within: Gnostic Readings in Marcel Proust, Flannery O'Connor, and François Villon* by Jefferson Humphries, © 1983 by Louisiana State University Press. Reprinted by permission.

"What You Can't Talk About" by John Burt, © 1986 by John Burt. Published for the first time in this volume. Printed by permission.

Index